WEDDING SHOWER FUN

by
SHARON E. DLUGOSCH
and
FLORENCE E. NELSON

with
SHOWERWISE

BRIGHTON PUBLICATIONS, INC.

Illustrations by Sandra T. Knuth
Word Processing by Nancy R. McCann

BRIGHTON PUBLICATIONS, INC.

Brighton Publications, Inc.
P.O. Box 12706
New Brighton, MN 55112
(612) 636-2220

First Edition: January 1984
Second Edition: May 1985
Third Edition: September 1986

Printed in the United States of America

Library of Congress Catalog
Card Number: 83-072952
International Standard Book Number:
0-918420-22-9

CONTENTS

BEFORE THE BEGINNING   8
Meet ShowerWise—Believe it or not!

DEAR SHOWERWISE   11
Surprising questions—Down-to-earth answers!

You shower givers and goers around the country came up with some party problems worth sharing. Here's the best of the batch—with solutions from ShowerWise!

BORED	11
TOO BUSY	12
FAMILY LOVER	12
SECOND TIME AROUND	13
STUDENT	13
ELEGANT	13
TIME, BUT NO MONEY	14
DRAMATIC	14
NEED TEMPORARY OFFICE HELP	14
NOT FOR WOMEN ONLY	15
DANCING, BUT NOT ON AIR	15
MOVING DILEMMA	16
NEED BETTER ODDS	16
DOWN WITH STAG PARTIES	17
POOR RELATIVE	17
WILLING, BUT CAN'T DECIDE	17
SENTIMENTAL	18
NEW WOMAN AND NEW MAN	19
HEALTH FOOD/DIETER NUT	19
HOLIDAY HANG-UP	19
MONEY, BUT NO TIME	20
PRACTICAL	20
NO GAMES	21
SHOWERS FOREVER	21
GOOD IMAGINATION	22
FAMILIES OF THE BETROTHED COUPLE	22
THE BRIDAL PARTY	22

Methods for come-alive showers!

Start with a comfortable theme and one you think will be fun for you and your guests. Casual or formal, traditional or unique—It's all here!

SHOW-ME SHOWER   24
SHOWER-ON-A-SHOESTRING SHOWER   26
WINE-AND-CHEESE-TASTING SHOWER   27
SUNDAY-GO-TO-MEETING SHOWER   29
POUNDING-PARTY SHOWER   31
FORMAL POOL SHOWER   33
HOME-FROM-THE-HONEYMOON SHOWER   35
COLLEGE SOAP-OPERA SHOWER   37
SECOND-TIME-AROUND SHOWER   39
COOKIE-SAMPLER SHOWER   41
HANDY-ANDY/HARDWARE-HANNAH SHOWER   42
APARTMENT/CONDO POOL SHOWER   44
ROAST-THE-MANAGER SHOWER   47
BE-MY-VALENTINE SHOWER   49
MEET-THE-RELATIVES SHOWER   51
THE ELEGANT SHOWER   53
DOLLAR-DISCO-DANCE SHOWER   55
TIE-A-QUILT SHOWER   57
OFFICE CO-WORKER SHOWER   60
SHARE-A-MENU SHOWER   61
SURPRISE-FRIENDSHIP SHOWER   63
CALORIE-COUNTER SHOWER   65
HOLLYWOOD STARS SHOWER   67
CO-HOSTESS SHOWER   69
NO-SWEAT SHOWER   71
ROMANTIC NOVEL SHOWER   73
WOK-ON-THE-WILD-SIDE SHOWER   74
GIFT-THEME GALLERY   76
   WEDDING REGISTRY SHOWER   77
   GREENHOUSE SHOWER   78
   POSTAL SHOWER   78
   CHERISHED-GIFT SHOWER   79
   LEND-A-HAND SHOWER   79
   GIFTS-AROUND-THE-CLOCK SHOWER   80

You're on your own!

Now that you've got the idea, here are twenty-four gems that can help you develop your own themes—all have A-1 ratings from ShowerWise!

COLLECTIBLE SHOWER   82
LAS VEGAS DICE-THROW SHOWER   83
CORNUCOPIA SHOWER   83
HERB-AND-SPICE SHOWER   83
CANDLELIGHT SHOWER   83
SHEET-MUSIC SHOWER   83
BIO-RHYTHM SHOWER   84
FABULOUS-FORTIES SHOWER   84
NIFTY-FIFTIES SHOWER   84
CHRISTMAS-BAUBLE SHOWER   85
HEALTH-FOOD-HARVEST SHOWER   85
OPEN-DOOR SHOWER   85
LET'S-GET-CANNED SHOWER   85
TAILGATE SHOWER   86
FILE-AND-FIND-IT SHOWER   86
 ∽ HERITAGE THEME GALLERY ∽   86
SCANDINAVIAN SHOWER   86
MEXICAN SHOWER   86
GERMAN SHOWER   87
ITALIAN SHOWER   87
HAWAIIAN SHOWER   87
ORIENTAL SHOWER   87
SONG-OF-INDIA SHOWER   88
ENGLISH-TEA SHOWER   88
ERIN-GO-BRAGH SHOWER   88

Take our hands and let's go!

Here's a little easy-to-take explanation and organization for
you that could mean the difference between a shower that's
drudgery or one that makes you shine—ShowerWise has
covered all the bases!

12 STEPS TO A SUCCESSFUL SHOWER   89
   Guests • Time • Theme • Location • Invitations •
   Food • Decoration • Games • Activities • Added
   Attractions • Helpers • Enjoy!
SHOWER PLANNING SHEET   92
SHARED SHOWER PROTOCOL   96
   For the Hostess or Host   96
   For the Intended Couple   97
THE WEDDING REGISTRY SERVICE   98

SHOWERWISE GUIDES   100
10 Guides to help you plan—A downpour of ideas . . . all
YOURS!

Here are ten timely guides full of ideas, methods, instructions and directions. Even if you never have a shower, you'll
use them to add that "extra something" to any occasion—
ShowerWise guarantees it!

ACTIVITIES GUIDE   100
   Ideas From Shower Themes   100
   Folding Table Napkins   101
INVITATIONS GUIDE   106
   Ideas from Shower Themes   107
   Other Ideas   107
   Printer Ready Invitations   109
DECORATIONS GUIDE   121
   Decorate Your Room Or Space   121
   Decorate Your Table   123
   Decorate Your Gift-Opening Area   125
      The Chair(s)-of-Honor   127
      The Honored Couple   127

Decorate Your Guests 129
FOOD-TABLE SET-UP GUIDE 130
Buffet Blueprint 130
Sit-Down Dinner Blueprint 131
Dessert-Only Blueprint 132
FAVORS, NAME TAG AND
 PLACE CARD GUIDE 133
Ideas From Shower Themes 133
Other Ideas 135
ADDED ATTRACTIONS GUIDE 136
Ideas From Shower Themes 136
Other Ideas 137
GIFT GUIDE 137
Party-Giver Gift 137
Ideas From Shower Themes 137
Other Ideas 138
GIFT-WRAP GUIDE 139
Ideas From Shower Themes 139
Other Ideas 139
PRIZES GUIDE 140
Kitchen Gadget Suggestions 140
Prize Suggestions For Men-Only Showers 140
Prize Suggestions For Women-Only Showers 140
Prize Suggestions For A Couples Shower 140
UNUSUAL LOCATIONS GUIDE 141
Ideas From Shower Themes 141
Other Ideas 141

AFTER THE END 142
Now do you believe it?

SPECIAL NOTE FROM SHOWERWISE 142
Guess who has the last word?

SHOWER THEME INDEX 143

BEFORE THE BEGINNING . . .

This book was written because neither of us particularly liked showers. For years, each of us kept this fact hidden under our umbrellas. Then, on a bright, sunny day, one of us said it out loud, "I HATE SHOWERS!" We can't tell you who voiced it because it was such a shock.

Well, we reasoned, if WE hate showers, that makes two. And if there are two of us, there must be more closet shower-haters. Well, indeed there were.

So, why a WEDDING SHOWER FUN book? Because we found an interesting phenomenon in talking with many women, and receiving the results of a shower survey we mailed to individuals and gift stores around the country. Even though there seemed to be a general, yet uneasy dislike for giving and going to showers, no one really wanted to banish the custom forever.

That presented a real dilemma because before results started to come in, we began preparing our "Down With Showers" posters. But more and more, we realized what people were actually saying. They talked about busy schedules, limited funds, wanting to include men and families and, in general, not really knowing just HOW to put on a shower-to-be-remembered.

Ah-ha! We had a clue. The riddle lay not in showers. They had pretty much stayed the same. It was us! Our busy lives, our love of activity, our new relationships with our men . . . we're the ones who'd changed. No wonder we'd gotten too big for our umbrellas!

Now you may find this hard to believe, but at that very instant, two very wise and wonderful li'l cupids (toting a shower umbrella!) perched on our desk. With a twirl of their parasol, they winked and said, "SHOWERWISE IS OUR NAME— FOND MEMORIES, OUR GAME!" Then and there, we knew we were on to something.

"You really don't hate showers," they told us.

"Ha!" we replied. "Then what's going on?"

"It's just that your lives have changed, but your shower giving and going hasn't. So many of you are working outside the home now there just isn't as much time available. And you do love your sports and activities! That's just fine because you're building strong, healthy bodies. But you see, that increases the time pinch even more. And how about the unsettling influence of the 60's? People began to look at the rituals surrounding the wedding in an entirely different way. Why, there's a whole generation of young people who don't even know HOW to put on a shower! "No, you don't hate 'em at all," they said, finally taking a breath. "You're just confused!"

Well, we had to admit ShowerWise had something there. We really do want to join with family and friends at this very special moment in their lives, when fond memories are being formed.

"Of course you do," said ShowerWise, reading our minds. "And one occasion that adds to this wonderful collection of memories is the wedding shower!"

"That's true," we replied, thoughtfully. "It sounds as if you have something on your minds. What do you suggest?"

"Well, first of all," they said in unison, "you've really done your homework. The survey you sent to women around the country brought back a lot of good information and ideas. Why, you've opened up a whole new shower world!''

For one solid minute they flapped their wings and flew up to the rafters and back again, over and over, turning somersaults along the way. We couldn't swear to it, but wedding bells seemed to be ringing, off in the distance.

Now is the time to act, we agreed. "As we see it," we said, finally bringing them back down to eye level, "we've got to turn all these obstacles around and use them to create a fun and easy party for ourselves, as well as for our guests.''

"Excellent! Excellent!" they shouted. "With what you know about showers from the results of your survey, and what we know about love and romance, we'd make a great team. Will you let us help?''

"Funny you should ask," we smiled, quite satisfied with ourselves.

Well, the rest is history. We tried to write everything down exactly as they said it. There's no doubt about it. Thanks to ShowerWise, our next shower's going to be a knock-out!

Sharon E. Dlugosch
Florence E. Nelson

DEAR SHOWERWISE

Did you know there's a Great-Wedding-Shower-Galaxy beyond the Milky Way? Yes, that's what ShowerWise both told us. It's a place where cupids can fly (in an instant) to get their inspiration ... just as we got ours from them.

Well, it didn't take us long to jot down every question we'd heard from people around the country. Could ShowerWise give us some answers? You bet they could ... and off they went!

Did we say in an instant? It didn't seem that long, but here they are now. So, find a cozy chair and settle back. You're in for some surprises.

DEAR SHOWERWISE:
Every shower's the same. Games, food and chatter. Isn't there anything new under the sun?

—Bored

DEAR "BORED,"
You can turn any shower into sunshine if you're willing to do something a bit different. For instance, in one part of the country, there's a new idea that's really taking hold— "Wine-And-Cheese-Tasting" showers. In another, "Show-Me" showers are gaining in popularity. One thing's for sure.

You're not alone in your boredom. So check out our SHOWERWISE THEMES for details of these two showers and for other ideas that may get you and your friends out of the shower blahs!

——————

DEAR SHOWERWISE:

I know I should, but how can I possibly give a shower for a close friend? My calendar is full.

—Too Busy

DEAR "BUSY,"

You won't have to miss a step! If you're too busy, it probably means you're involved in many activities. Chances are at least one of these must include your close friend, or you wouldn't be close for long . . . you'd never see each other! One of these activities could be the germ of a shower theme. Read our "No-Sweat," "Tie-A-Quilt," and "Calorie-Counter" showers for openers. These are all examples of bringing the shower to the group, instead of the other way around. Or to put it another way, they make the shower a part of YOUR life, not your life a part of the shower.

——————

DEAR SHOWERWISE:

I'd really like to see my whole family take part in the shower custom. Do you have any idea how we can pull it off?

—Family Lover

DEAR "LOVER,"

Why not? We find children especially love these occasions and will treasure such memories for a long time. If you're part of a religious community, our "Sunday-Go-To-Meeting" shower may be what you're looking for. Alternate choices might be our "Open-Door" or "Dollar-Disco-Dance" showers. And if you're not into disco dancing, use the same theme idea around polka or ballroom dancing. Ah-one an ah-two!

DEAR SHOWERWISE:

This is a second marriage for both of us—and really, we have all we need. It would be nice to just celebrate with our friends.

—Second Time Around

DEAR "SECOND TIME,"

A new start very often makes us want to create entirely different memory patterns. Our "Second-Time-Around" shower was meant for couples like you. It's based on an actual shower we attended and really enjoyed. We think you'll enjoy it too.

━━━━━

DEAR SHOWERWISE:

Between all our different college class schedules and tight budgets, how can I possibly give a shower for my roommate?

—Student

DEAR "STUDENT,"

We deserve an "A" for coming up with this one! Now here's your chance to make the grade. What's the one time of day you're all together, no matter what? You've got it! . . . during your favorite Soap Opera, and that's what we've named this theme. For a quieter, more tender time, see our "Tie-A-Quilt" shower, too. Homemakers take note. Instead of a soap opera coffee break, shift the scene and make it a "Soap-Opera" shower break.

━━━━━

DEAR SHOWERWISE:

Everything must be just right. My guests have to leave believing they never have, and never will, attend a shower like the one I host.

—Elegant

DEAR "ELEGANT,"

For rave reviews, plan carefully and pay close attention to detail. Off the top of our brows, we can think of two humdingers—ahem . . . that is, two splendid—ideas. The "Elegant" shower was created just for you. Do read that theme first. Our "Formal Pool" shower is in a class of its own and most impressive.

DEAR SHOWERWISE:

I want to give a shower for my best friend, but it's a little embarrassing. I find myself with limited funds for such an affair. I'm willing to work . . .

—Time, But No Money

DEAR "TIME,"

Showers do take money, but not necessarily yours. Our "Shower-On-A-Shoestring" and "Co-Hostess" showers are a good example of this, but there are many other ideas. In some places, it's practically a tradition to share the work, time AND money. Our "College Soap-Opera" and "Tie-A-Quilt" showers can also fill the bill when the green stuff is in short supply.

DEAR SHOWERWISE:

Every shower I've ever attended has been the same old thing. I want to do something REALLY different!

—Dramatic

DEAR "DRAMATIC,"

Are you ready for us? How about transporting your guests to Gothic times with our "Romantic Novel" shower? Or maybe stardom appeals to you. It's all "lights, camera, action!" in our "Hollywood Stars" shower. What could be more dramatic than a melodrama or a celebrity hoe-down? That's show biz!

DEAR SHOWERWISE:

Whenever someone in my office is getting married, nobody seems to know what to do about gifting and putting on a shower. Another one's coming up soon . . . S.O.S.!

—Need Temporary Office Help

DEAR "TEMPORARY,"

Back to basics! See SHOWERWISE STEPS for our "12 Steps To A Successful Shower," and also our "Shower Planning Sheet." Now you didn't say where you are on the office ladder, so we'll give you two helpful ideas. "Office Co-Worker" and "Roast-the-Manager" showers should promote your climb to successful showers.

———

DEAR SHOWERWISE:

Is there any chance we can get men interested in the traditionally all female shower?

—Not For Women Only

DEAR "NOT,"

You've hit on the latest trend! Many couples feel the same way and they're doing something about it. In general, you'll find that some kind of activity will "hook" the male element. Our "Wok-On-The-Wild-Side" and "Apartment/Condo Pool" showers provide that hooker. More sneaky ideas in SHOWERWISE THEMES and SHOWERWISE SPRINKLES.

———

DEAR SHOWERWISE:

There's a bride-to-be in my jazzercise class and we'd like to give her a shower. Trouble is, we're having a hard time finding a night or week-end we're all free.

—Dancing, But Not On Air

DEAR "DANCING,"

Believe it or not, you don't have a problem! Keep your leotard on and leap to the locker room right after class. More surprises for you figure conscious ones in our "No Sweat" and "Calorie-Counter" showers. Take a peek at our "Tailgate" shower in SHOWERWISE SPRINKLES, too. See . . . no problem at all!

DEAR SHOWERWISE:

The bride and groom are moving to another state right after their wedding and won't have room for extra baggage. We thought of sending gifts to their new address, but we'd like to share a shower memory with them before they leave. Any ideas?

—Moving Dilemma

DEAR "DILEMMA,"

We'll give you a hint. There's a certain gift that's lightweight, desired by almost everyone, requires no shopping . . . and is definitely portable! Have we stumped you? See our "Dollar-Disco-Dance" shower for details. One which may not require gifts at all is our "Surprise-Friendship" shower. It could mean even more to the couple if the circumstances are right. Both showers will send them off to their new state with happy memories.

DEAR SHOWERWISE:

I want to have a shower, but everyone I know either hates showers or is so busy. How can I be sure that enough people will come?

—Need Better Odds

DEAR "BETTER ODDS,"

A little bait should do the trick. You can make your shower seem so intriguing that people will forego other plans and attitudes to attend. Choosing an unusual theme, possibly one that brings the party to the people, is the first step. Then create anticipation with a dramatic invitation. You'll find ideas in our INVITATIONS GUIDE. Then, get ready for a full house!

——————

DEAR SHOWERWISE:

How can we include men in our next shower? After THEIR parties it seems she's mad, her parents are nervous . . . and he's hung over.

—Down With Stag Parties

DEAR "DOWN,"

Any relationship should have a better start than that. How does our "Handy-Andy/Hardware-Hannah" shower sound? This is one that can also be given by the groom's friends or Father, in PLACE of the stag party. For couples, we think our "Wok-On-The-Wild-Side" and "Wine-And-Cheese-Tasting" showers work nicely. Good beginnings are guaranteed.

——————

DEAR SHOWERWISE:

Most showers are such a mixture of people, you never get a chance to find out who the rich relatives are.

—Poor Relative

DEAR "POOR,"

Delve into our FAVORS GUIDE where you'll find good ideas for name tags. When these are well done, such as "Pillow Puff" and "Rosebud," they also serve as a treasured keepsake. Hence, they do double duty: a name tag AND a favor. As you'll notice, we go a little further than most name tags by also stating the relationship of the guest to the couple. We're sure a few discreet inquiries on your part will uncover any rich aunts and uncles!

——————

DEAR SHOWERWISE:

Gifts are my problem. I never know what to purchase and I'm usually so busy, I can't spend time browsing through stores. I need a good . . . no, a GREAT solution.

—Willing, But Can't Decide

DEAR "WILLING,"

Browse no more! Are you familiar with the "Wedding Registry" (also called the "Bridal Registry")? Here's the process: the couple registers their gift preferences at a department or gift store. These can be anything from everyday dishes, decorative items and linens to china and small appliances. Trained salespeople counsel them in their choices and encourage selections in all price ranges. Gift-givers can visit or call these stores to make a speedy selection, and one they know the couple will enjoy and won't return! How's that for GREAT?

━━━━━

DEAR SHOWERWISE:

My parents never had a shower because they eloped. Now, some good friends have suddenly decided to marry next month. I know time is short, but I don't want them to miss out on a memory.

—Sentimental

DEAR "SENTIMENTAL,"

You're the tender stuff friends are made of. Why not make it easy on the harried couple and plan our "Home-From-The-Honeymoon" shower? If conditions are right and you can pull it off, our "Surprise Friendship" shower would also be a nice touch. By the way, it's not too late to shower your parents, either. Chances are, the relatives would get a bang out of it, too. Our "Dollar-Disco-Dance" shower could give them a second honeymoon.

DEAR SHOWERWISE:

Why are showers just for women? Leaving men out goes against our philosophy. To us, marriage is a shared endeavor in all ways.

—New Woman And New Man

DEAR "NEW,"

You're definitely in synch with the future. The truth is, many couples around the country feel as you do and are quietly making changes. Judging from our mail, there's hardly a need to be hush-hush about it anymore. In many places it's becoming the norm. So, go to it! Choose any of our couples' showers for your debut. "Wok-On-The-Wild-Side," "Wine-And-Cheese-Tasting" and "Apartment/Condo Pool" are just three you might consider for the togetherness you want.

DEAR SHOWERWISE:

Showers to me and most of my friends mean just another dose of junk food and adding weight we've so desperately been trying to lose. Why must fun times include so many forbidden foods?

—Health Food/Dieter Nut

DEAR "NUT,"

You have lots of company! Dieting is very much on people's minds. And when we see the attempt large food companies are making to develop wholesome foods, it has to mean people are becoming conscious of their bodies and what goes into them. Why not look over our "Calorie-Counter" shower in SHOWERWISE THEMES and "Health-Food-Harvest" shower in SHOWERWISE SPRINKLES? Healthy can be fun, too.

DEAR SHOWERWISE:

When wedding dates fall near a holiday, is it too tacky to tie in the shower with the holiday?

—Holiday Hang-Up

DEAR "HANG-UP,"

Actually, it's a good spot to be in. Decorating is simplified and you've got a ready-made theme. For ideas, see our "Be-My-Valentine" shower in SHOWERWISE THEMES and our "Christmas-Baubles" shower in SHOWERWISE SPRINKLES. Hold the shower BEFORE the holiday when anticipation is high. There's one exception. The week between Christmas and New Year's Day is still timely. With most other holidays, the 'thrill' and impact are gone ... like eating yesterday's cold potatoes.

━━━━━

DEAR SHOWERWISE:

I don't care what it costs! I only have a limited amount of time to plan and give a shower. What have you got for me?
—Money, But No Time

DEAR "MONEY,"

Lucky you! You can take your pick. All you need is one of our SHOWERWISE THEMES and a telephone. Our "Elegant" and "Formal Pool" showers can solve your problem. And if you haven't time for phoning, pick a date, hand our plan to your caterer or a professional party service ... and hand the bills to your accountant!

━━━━━

DEAR SHOWERWISE:

So many showers are all fluff and many of the gifts are useless. How can I diplomatically steer guests into purchasing a useful gift?
—Practical

DEAR "PRACTICAL,"

Your question reminds us of the bride-to-be who opened a shower gift and exclaimed, "Oh, how lovely" ... then desperately whispered to her mother, "What IS it?" The obvious solution is the "Wedding Registry" shower (see our "Gift-Theme Gallery" in SHOWERWISE THEMES). Even if the gift seems ridiculous to you, at least you'll know it was the couple's selection. Some new ideas are our "Handy-

Andy/Hardware Hannah" and "Pounding-Party" showers.
Strictly useful gifts, fun . . . and no fluff!

—————

DEAR SHOWERWISE:

Honestly, I don't want to play another dumb shower game!
Fill my precious time with something worthwhile.

—No Games

DEAR "NO GAMES,"

Throw away your pencil and dice forever! What you need
are activities, not games. We think our "Show-Me" and
"Cookie-Sampler" showers would really appeal to you.
"Show-Me" is a capsule version of the how-to classes that are
sweeping the country. You might also look over our ACTIVI-
TIES GUIDE. Most themes can be adapted for any shower
. . . and you'll never have to play another game!

—————

DEAR SHOWERWISE:

I just love giving showers! We have the best time, but I'm
out of fresh ideas. Can you help?

—Showers Forever

DEAR "FOREVER,"

Hold on to your umbrella! You'll find many fresh and re-
freshing ideas in our SHOWERWISE THEMES. We think
you'll especially like our "Greenhouse" and "Show-Me"
showers. Be sure to consider our "Share-A-Menu" and "Tie-
A-Quilt" showers and look over our "Gift-Theme Gallery"
in that section also. Do you know you're a wedding couple's
dream?

DEAR SHOWERWISE:

Don't tell me what to do! Just give me the germ of an idea and let me take it from there.

—Good Imagination

DEAR "IMAGINATION,"

We have a whole section for you. They're not complete showers in themselves . . . just ideas and suggestions you can build on. Actually, they're more like sprinkles. And that's what we've called them . . . SHOWERWISE SPRINKLES. Read them through and let your imagination take off. You're on your own!

—■—■—■—

DEAR SHOWERWISE:

Because we'll be connected in the future, we'd like both families of the wedding couple to get to know each other a little better. How can we do this without the usual strain and pain involved when 'strangers' try to do a social number?

—Families Of The Betrothed Couple

DEAR "FAMILIES,"

We've got a pretty clever trick up our sleeves for you. It can do more to put everyone at ease on this occasion than a talk show host. Try our "Meet-The-Relatives" shower. No strain . . . and definitely, no pain!

—■—■—■—

DEAR SHOWERWISE:

Our shower has only one requirement. We want it to be the start of many warm and wonderful memories for our favorite wedding couple.

—The Bridal Party

DEAR "BRIDAL PARTY,"

We hear you loud and clear! You echo the words of wedding parties around the country who'd all like to honor 'their' couple in a very special way. Well, this book is for you! You'll find over fifty workable ideas to choose from. Any one of them will help you give a special shower filled with warm and wonderful memories.

SHOWERWISE THEMES

"It's very important"...and we're quoting Shower-Wise, here, "to help people understand that any of the following shower ideas can be blended with others or with their own ideas." So don't feel locked into following one theme specifically, though you can. Mix and match until you get a fit just right for you.

We're supposed to tell you, too, that even though Shower-Wise may say, "This is a good couples shower" for a particular theme, adapt the idea to your own needs: couples, mixed couples, singles, women only, men only, or families.

ShowerWise also wants you to know that you'll find something very different here. We've made a distinction between "Games," "Activities" and "Added Attractions."

GAMES have been the mainstay of showers for a long, long time. They give people who may be strangers something to do and can create an element of fun. Several can be found in our publication, GAMES FOR WEDDING SHOWER FUN, along with game sheets, so they won't be repeated here.

ACTIVITIES, on the other hand, are our very own new addition to the shower custom. Rather than separating the shower into sections (food, games, gifts), they tend to pull all the parts together. Besides giving guests something to DO, they also give them something to focus on, to put them at ease and help conversation flow. In general, they help people with different lives and interests find a common ground to have fun together for a limited period of time.

ADDED ATTRACTIONS are those special effects that give added sparkle and flair to any event. They may be combined with games or activities, or stand on their own. Added Attractions range from something as simple as background music to a synchronized-swim performance.

Thumb through all our themes and guides to guarantee an exciting and amusing shower you and your guests will enjoy and remember. Just think of the possibilities! But, don't think too long. These shower themes are meant to be used.

 # SHOW-ME SHOWER

This shower is an outstanding example of one of our "activity" themes. It gives people something constructive to DO and eliminates the need for contrived entertainment. Many people love showers, just as they are. However, in our survey we noticed a growing number who said, "No more games!" and "Give me something to DO!". If this is the case in your area, you may want to try something different.

Do you or one of your friends have a special talent that can easily be shared with your guests? Are there any cake decorators, craftspeople or gourmet cooks in the group? Holding a short, how-to session, with everyone taking part, can be fun for all.

In Minnesota, we held a napkin folding demonstration that was very successful. This subject lends itself particularly well because instructions are simple, inexpensive paper napkins can be used, and every age group and gender seems to enjoy it. People like joining together for a talking, laughing and DOING good time.

Here's how you can make an eye-catching invitation. Fold a paper napkin into an attractive napkin fold, write your invitation on the completed fold, tuck it into your envelope and mail. A simple napkin fold for this purpose can be found in our INVITATIONS GUIDE. Other folds named in this theme can be found in our ACTIVITIES GUIDE.

For the actual how-to demonstration, we've chosen four folds that should serve the couple well during their first year: The Cascade for their Wedding Table, The Cactus for their First Breakfast, the Palm Leaf for their First Dinner Party, and The Rose for their First Anniversary Dinner.

Provide your guests with plenty of variously colored paper napkins so they can work right along with the demonstrator. Allowing time for the usual chatter and laughter you hear when people are having a good time, the demonstration should take about 30 minutes. The completed folds become instant favors for your guests.

Though we've turned the spotlight on napkin folding here, other subjects would work equally well. Some that lend themselves are: cake decorating, flower arranging, silk flower making, simple macrame wall hangings or personal accessories.

If you'd like to bring in someone from the outside to demonstrate, call the community education department at your local high school. They'll be glad to suggest one or two of their instructors. Try your local gift shop too, especially if that's where the couple's wedding registry is recorded.

And there you have it! Coupled with a simple dessert menu and gift-opening, your shower can be the talk of the town . . . or should we say, the dinner table!

SHOWER-ON-A-SHOESTRING

This shower is practically a tradition in some parts of the country. A cooperative effort, the emphasis is on food and food-related gifts, with guests very much taking part in the planning. It works especially well for friends who've set an entertaining pattern together, or who wish to honor the off-spring of a neighbor.

This coordinated "potluck" activity has each guest bringing a food item in a serving container that will become a gift for the honored guest. After the food is served, everyone joins in to wash and dry the gift pieces. At gift time, each guest tucks a gift card into the appropriate gift, along with the recipe that was used. If additional gifts are desired, baskets to hold the serving dishes, hot pads, serving utensils, or a basic recipe ingredient may be added.

This shower spreads the work, time and cost around, but requires one meeting of all or most of the guests at least three weeks beforehand. At this time, you should plan the entire shower and make all major decisions of date, location, time, menu, decorations, etc. The rest can be done by telephone. Because of this, invitations are rarely sent.

In creating a festive atmosphere throughout the shower area, don't forget the kitchen. Since it's important to the theme, you may want to do something special here. Aside from that, you'll find good ideas for the table, gift-opening area and general atmosphere in our DECORATIONS GUIDE.

A good activity idea came to us from Arlene Hamernik, a Fridley, Minnesota Home Economist. She suggests you make a corsage from ribbon and netting. But instead of using flowers, just fasten small unusual kitchen items to it (strawberry huller, tea infuser, pastry brush, etc.). As you present it to the bride, ask her to explain how each item is used . . . with no coaching from the audience.

Besides the good food and fellowship this shower provides, it's an excellent opportunity to supply the couple with the serving pieces they desire. Of course, gift purchasing is much easier if they've chosen their patterns through a wedding registry at a gift shop. You'll have a choice of china, everyday pieces, glassware and many other items. If you want to give additional gifts, use your ingenuity to spot pieces that aren't necessarily for table service. Ash trays can hold celery sticks and olives, while oven mitts can double as utensil packets for an attractive shower buffet.

All in all, this is what we'd call an "easy-going" occasion. Once the planning and initial work is done, everyone can relax and have a pleasant time.

ANOTHER IDEA: 1) Progressive Dinner (especially in apartment/condo setting or within a neighborhood). Bring gift serving pieces to the dessert location and wash them there. 2) Picnic. Arrangements should be made for a place to wash dishes. National Parks, and some local parks, usually have these facilities.

WINE-AND-CHEESE- TASTING SHOWER

A real lifestyle shower—or something just a bit different—this one adds a little merriment to the occasion. It's a good way to stock the wedding couple's bar, too. Your taste buds will ask that you sample no more than five or six wines . . . for tasting and merriment reasons! Cheeses, of course, are a different story.

So let's stock the bar and have some fun! Find out if the couple's preference runs to the red or white wines. Ask each guest to bring two gift bottles of the same wine. One is gift-wrapped, with gift card attached. The other is used for the wine tasting activity. Since wine is not a lasting gift, guests may wish to bring an additional, wine-related item. Good selections are a carafe, corkscrew, a good wine book, wine making kit, an apron with wine slogan, or a set of wine glasses inscribed with the couple's names and wedding date. Visit your local liquor store, or one of the wine shops that have become so popular, for other gift ideas.

Planning this shower around the cocktail hour should be enough to lure your guests. But if you feel the need for more enticement, how about designing a mock wine label invitation, as illustrated. Choose a favorite label and duplicate it, leaving room for date, time, etc. Or for a really dramatic effect, write your invitation on plastic wine glasses! Neatly box them in pillows of tissue paper and mail ... or hand deliver.

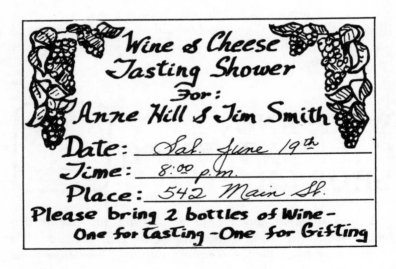

Now that all guests are assembled, what's the procedure? You can check with your favorite liquor or wine store manager, or follow these simple guidelines.

Bring on each wine and cheese selection as a set, one set at a time. Rinse out glasses between tasting. For refreshment variety, also serve crusty French bread or crackers with fresh fruit slices. Be sure to make club soda and plenty of water available. These cleanse the palate, rest the taste buds, and prevent TOO much merriment.

Before each wine is tested, ask guests to offer a favorite toast to the wedding couple. Toasting words can be used for emphasis: PROSIT!(German), SANTE!(French), SALUTE! (Italian), SKOAL!(Swedish), PROOST!(Dutch), SALUD! (Spanish)...and CHEERS!

Between wine courses, have the intended couple "test" their kitchen arts by washing and drying all glasses. Of course, guests make it a point to stand on the sidelines, offering suggestions and poking good-natured fun at the couple's cooperative effort.

When you decorate your service table, plan a spot for a wine rack large enough to hold all wrapped wine bottles. As guests arrive with their gifts, insert them into a slot and your table becomes more and more festive...just like magic!

Appropriate for couples, singles or mixed singles groups, this unusual shower is an alternative. If you've got the lifestyle, the friends, and the inclination to do something different, chances are before the night is over, they'll be toasting YOU!

SUNDAY-GO-TO-MEETING SHOWER

Here's an "open house" type shower for a popular church member or couple. It's held right after services and announced at least two weeks before the event in the bulletin or at services. All members' families are invited, so men and children are definitely part of the festivities. You'll be able to enlist lots of person-power for planning, food preparation and cleaning up . . . a real plus!

In Dallas, Texas, Lynn Wheeler tells us that church members hold showers by sharing the work "round robin" style. Eight hostesses serve at each one, with the list rotating. Finger sandwiches, cake, cookies, coffee and punch are served. They've got it down to a science in Dallas and their fellowship hall sees lots of action.

Many church communities, especially the smaller ones, have the same shower custom. If your church already has a system, you may want to incorporate some of our ideas. If it doesn't, maybe you can start this time-honored custom in your area.

One of the nicest activities we've heard of for this shower is a variation of the prayer circle. In this case, guests hold hands, forming a "CONGRATULATORY" circle. The bride and groom stand in the center and all remarks are addressed to them. A close friend starts with a few words of instruction, to set the tone. The person on his or her right takes it from there and so on around, until everyone has been heard from . . . even the children. The words are simple: "congratulations," "lots of happiness," "I love you," "I wish you the best," etc. Once again, it's back to the friend, who puts a final, tender touch on the bevy of wishes. Then everyone swoops in toward the couple for handshaking, hugs and kisses. Plan this activity as soon as everyone has assembled and before refreshments are served.

In Missouri, selected members of the church choir serenade the couple with appropriate love songs. This is a touching moment for the intended bride and groom and also entertainment for the whole group.

In Washington, guests write a few words of advice in a special blank book. Remarks are both serious and humorous, centered around ways to help the couple keep their religious cool in a secular world.

In New Jersey, polaroid photos of the occasion are slipped into an album on the spot. This supplies the couple with a special remembrance gift.

In most churches, this shower is an occasion that re-affirms the marriage contract and provides the couple with gifts to help them enhance their spiritual life. A family Bible, a subscription to religious magazines or newspapers, a wall plaque, and an anniversary candle are among those that are appropriate.

A buffet lunch served from a nicely decorated table caps the shower. Guests extend their best wishes as the couple circulate around the room, and once again we've brought the shower to the people. Whoever said, "NEVER ON SUNDAY?"

POUNDING-PARTY SHOWER

Here's a shower for the practical-minded. After all, what marriage hasn't been enhanced by a pound of sugar and a pound of nails? Loosely adapted from the custom of welcoming the new preacher into town, it gives the couple a very nice start. When a short, fun-filled verse accompanies each present, gift-opening becomes the activity here.

A pound of what? Well, in those days, any food staple was welcomed. The parson and his family most likely arrived in town with a few clothes, some furniture, and very little else. When you think about it, that's the way many couples start their married lives today. This shower changes all that and injects a bit of fun to boot.

We suggest you scour your neighborhood grocery, hardware, drug and stationery stores. Some unlikely items are sold by the pound. Here are a few we found as we searched. When combined with an obvious gift, and a few wise words of advice to the couple, you've got the makings of a laughter-filled, and, sometimes, tender shower:

1) A pound of Semolina flour with a pasta maker—"Think pasta-tively and have a happy marriage!"

2) A pound of mixed nuts with a nutcracker and dish—"You two nuts have a crackin' good life together!"

3) A pound of notepaper with a set of pens—"Always keep in touch with each other!"

Other ideas are coffee with a coffee maker, sugar with a cookie jar, rock salt with an ice cream maker, flour with a baking pan set, a pound loaf of bread with a bread box, and potato chips with a lazy susan.

Get the idea? We've suggested some free verse that you might share with your guests in a pinch. But the fun really begins when remarks are impromptu. So we suggest you wait until gift time to announce the procedure. The rule is: the gift can't be passed around for everyone to see until someone comes up with a few fitting words. Or you might give a prize to the person who creates the best verse for each gift. Let your guests decide the winners.

You'll find that one funny comment leads to another and you may even have to set a time limit! A mock "Laugh-Ah-Meter" (as illustrated—see directions in our SHOWER-WISE GUIDES) could spur things on ... "Laugh" for the

witty ones, "Ah" for the tender tidbits. All it takes is a half-circle of cardboard with a dial on it. Then just insert a clasp clip to hold the dial. As remarks are offered, you can move the hand from behind to estimate the group's reaction.

Now, one more consideration. Your invitation must give guests a good idea of what is expected in the way of gifts. As you can see, each present should be paired with a related "pound". The printer-ready copy in our INVITATION GUIDE is designed to get their creative juices flowing. Don't be surprised to find that when your guests leave, they'll either be quoting the great philosophers, or rhyming "Moon" and "June!" . . . by the pound!

ANOTHER IDEA: Sheila McGinn-Moorer of Evanston, Illinois, suggests filling a small suitcase with pennies. Guests try to guess the number of coins inside . . . or for our purposes . . . how many "pounds" the loaded case weighs. This is one time the wedding couple won't mind putting on the pounds. After the guessing is done and a prize awarded, the case and pennies become a surprise gift for them.

FORMAL POOL SHOWER

If you have an outdoor pool, or access to one, the sheer elegance of this shower will captivate your guests. The pool is the focal point, enhanced by the performance of a local synchronized-swim group, who literally decorate the pool during their show . . . right before your eyes! Get ready for ooh's, aah's and bravos!

Plan at least two months ahead so the swim group has time to practice their made-to-order routine. To find such a group, one of these contacts should be successful: swimming coach—local high school; aquatic director—YWCA, YMCA; swimming director—college or university; swimming coach—country club or health spa.

Hire the group to make all props and costumes, as well as to perform. Give them a good idea of what you expect and let them take it from there. Experienced swimmers know many routines. It will simply be a matter of combining various swim strokes, stunts and graceful maneuvers to decorate your pool and to provide delightful entertainment.

One romantic water sequence we like is performed in the evening, to the song, "Some Enchanted Evening". The swimmers appear from the shallow end of the pool carrying a large, heart-shaped form (cut from 3/4", 4' x 8' styrofoam). In the center of it is a spray of flowers, with a shower umbrella decoration. Colorful, wide ribbons are arranged to come out from underneath the flower centerpiece to the edge of the heart, spoke style. At the end of each ribbon is a large plastic bowl-type candleholder with candle inside (the kind used in restaurants and available from restaurant supply houses), secured with floral clay (as illustrated).

As the music starts, one swimmer lights the candles, then takes his or her place in the group. The heart is eased into the water, along with the swimmers, and the magic begins. Down the pool they go, in graceful strokes, gently taking the shower float with them. In the pool's deep end they use the heart as a center for all their stunts and strokes, appearing and disappearing, arms and legs in unison. At the climax, they fan out, each having removed a candleholder from the heart in order to place it along the edge of the pool, amid garlands of fresh flowers. For a surprising anti-climax, the heart is swum back to the shallow end, eased out of the pool, and set on a large tabletop. We told you it was magic. And there you have it . . . a perfect centerpiece for the refreshment table! But we're not done yet. As the feast is being laid out, all the swimmers but one dive into the pool and swim back to the edge to retrieve sparklers (as used on the 4th of July) that were nestled earlier in the flower garlands. They're quickly lighted by the remaining swimmer and the group executes one more snappy routine for a spectacular ending!

But that's not the end of your shower. Remember, lovely is the key word and the pace has been set with a romantic water dance. Everything else should be in keeping with this tone—formal dress, comfortable seating, dramatically served food, and gracious hosting.

ANOTHER IDEA: Suppose you don't want to tackle a swim show? You'll still have the makings of a lovely shower setting by following the idea for our heart-shaped float. Anchor it in the center of your pool and arrange spot lighting along the edge of the deck, illuminating the float.

HOME-FROM-THE HONEYMOON SHOWER

Held immediately following the honeymoon, this shower is especially appropriate for the couple who eloped or decided to marry rather quickly. It's a nice way to welcome the couple home while the occasion is still timely. It's also an opportunity for friends and family to get to know the half of the couple they didn't know too well in the hasty preparations (if any) before the wedding.

Besides seeing their families and friends, what do you think the couple would like most? What might they be hankering for after eating in restaurants morning, noon and night? Right . . . a good, home-cooked, cozy, sit-down dinner! We're calling the meal the activity for this shower because everything will revolve around it. Not that the menu has to be elaborate. On the contrary, a light supper is fine, just so it's home-cooked. But this is when most of the conversation will flow and you should plan around it.

Because this shower works well as a surprise, some good friends, or a member of either family, can invite the couple over for dinner soon after they return. Encourage them to bring their wedding photo proofs, snapshots taken on their honeymoon and souvenirs they collected along the way.

Ask the couple's parents to put together some of their baby and growing-up years photos, and perhaps some short home movies. Friends can also contribute from their snapshot albums and high school or college yearbooks and pictures they took at the wedding.

As you can see, we'll be reminiscing a great deal. It's a simple way to pull the past together for the couple who has joined in haste. It can help give them a solid base on which to build and let them know they have your support.

So let's welcome them home in style! When they enter the shower area and hear the shouts of "Surprise!", try to really bowl them over. Hand lettered "Welcome Home!" and "Just Married!" signs can be taped around the party room. Lots of balloons and string confetti will help create the effect you're looking for. And to top off the affair, reserve a place on the serving table for a "Welcome Home From The Honeymoon" decorated cake with all your guests names inscribed on it.

Go all out on decorating. Maria Nelson of St. Paul, Minnesota, suggests buying a large poster board and printing

"Marriage Advice From Your Family And Friends" across the top. Each guest is encouraged to write a few fun phrases on it during the shower. The couple is instructed to "meditate" over it every day. Make them a mock top-hat and bridal veil too (see our DECORATIONS GUIDE).

This shower is liable to be overwhelming for the couple. It would be nice if someone could stay close by to give them a bit of behind the scenes help, should they need it—refer to our "Shared Shower Protocol" section in SHOWERWISE STEPS. Overwhelming or not, we'll bet you'll have just as much fun as they will as you welcome them back to reality!

ANOTHER IDEA: In Fridley, Minnesota, Judy Simko tells us they include friends, relatives and their families on a Sunday afternoon for a light supper shower and a few games in which everyone can participate.

COLLEGE SOAP-OPERA SHOWER

Miss seeing your favorite soap to go to a shower? Never! Never! Never! So, there's only one thing to do. Switch on the tube and have a bring-your-own-lunch-or-snack shower in the student lounge or a dorm room. It's the time of day when you know everyone will be there anyhow, so there's no juggling of hours to find a perfect time.

A week or two before your shower event, create excitement by passing the word along via word-of-mouth, stressing the fact that NO ONE has to give up soap-opera time to attend. Get as many people as possible in on planning, making decorations, and purchasing the minimal supplies needed. It's a way of sharing the work and the cost . . . and having a good time together.

Decorations can be homemade and simple. One idea is to cut out pictures of soap opera characters from a fan magazine and paste head shots (photos) of the bride and groom over the faces of the stars. Naturally, these would adorn the TV set. Another idea is to make a mock top-hat and bridal veil from construction paper, foil and netting (see directions in our DECORATIONS GUIDE).

One goofy, active game after the soap should round out the shower nicely and will probably be all you'll have time for. If you're short on goofy, active games, here's one we think you'll enjoy. It's called the "shoe-box-shake" and comes from Linda Strohbeen of Shoreview, Minnesota. Fill two shoe boxes with clothespins, half of which have been X'd with nail polish or marker. Cut an opening in each box cover, twice the size of a clothespin. Attach ribbon or rope to each end of the shoeboxes, long enough to circle the average hip, and tie. At game time, tie the shoe boxes around two guests at a time, with the boxes resting on their backsides. Turn on the stereo and s-h-a-k-e. The person to empty the most clothespins in 30 seconds gets to keep all of them!

Perhaps goofy is not your bag. Maybe you're the intellectual types. If you put your heads together, we're sure you can create your own soap opera, centered around the courtship, wedding and happy life-ever-after of the couple you're showering. Each guest can read a portion of it . . . with proper emoting, of course. Be sure to make a tape recording of your scenario and take plenty of photos. Both are a nice remembrance for the couple.

The last activity for your shower is really the best part. It's similar to the custom of throwing rice at the couple after the wedding ceremony. However, you're going to ... not throw, but blow ... what else? ... SOAP bubbles at them. So supply each guest with a child's jar of soap bubbles, pucker up and give it all you've got for a grand and glorious "soap" finale!

SECOND-TIME- AROUND SHOWER

The thing that makes this shower so romantic is that the couple have gone through life's ups and downs and have found love again. Any one of the shower themes can be adapted for this occasion, but the one we attended was quite simple, yet elegant.

Since many second-timers begin their life together with two sets of everything, they don't need "things" to get them started. Some prefer instead to turn the tables, stating in the invitation—"No gifts, please ... Just loving friends and relatives to share our new-found joy." Rather than a shower of gifts, it becomes a shower of warm wishes. Yes, it's a real departure from the usual shower-giving situation.

It's appropriate when a small wedding is planned and most of the shower guests will not be invited. It's also a good way to thank family, friends and business associates for their past support in whatever circumstances surrounded the couple's first marriages, be it death or divorce.

This event may be held before or after the wedding. The location is determined by the number of guests and would work equally well in the home, in a country club setting or a hotel meeting room. There isn't much we could say to improve on the affair we attended—it was that good. So we've decided to describe it for you here, down to the last detail.

It was held in a lovely banquet room of a very nice hotel ... but there was no banquet. Instead, an elaborate hors d'oeuvres table greeted guests as they entered. The center-piece was an ice sculptured cupid with hands stretched downward, toward the food. It seemed to be saying, "Behold ... see the feast prepared for you ... Come cele-brate!" And, even though it consisted entirely of appetizers, it was indeed a feast: chicken wings, finger sausages, shrimp, tiny barbecued meatballs, cheeses, enormous relish and fruit trays, and an assortment of bread sticks and din-ner rolls. It was held during the cocktail hour so cham-pagne, wine and soft drinks were served.

In the background, a harpist played and was relieved during intermission by two violin players. They alternated during the evening, so there was always soft, unobtrusive music that seemed to carry over to the conversations we heard. Lovely, lilting friendship words and phrases filled the air.

The bride and groom stayed side by side, moving about the room to greet and say a few words to each of their guests. When the room seemed crowded to capacity, the couple asked for quiet by tapping a spoon against a glass. Each said a few words to the group, thanking them for attending and sharing their good fortune. Then they raised their champagne glasses and proposed a very tender, en-dearing toast to their guests. Believe us, there wasn't a person in the entire room who didn't feel very special!

From the formal, custom-printed invitation requesting no gifts, to the heartwarming toast finale, this shower was a real departure from custom. And yet, it worked beautifully. This couple had the courage to fit the custom to the circum-stances and everyone benefited. If your situation is unusual, don't be afraid to try something different. If this couple hadn't, we wouldn't have this five-year-old memory, now.

ANOTHER IDEA: Olga Iacobucci of Newtown Square, Pennsylvania, also departed from custom. Although it's common practice in her area for a member of the family to hold a shower, she went one step further. She invited forty young women ... and also invited the groom, her son. The wedding couple opened gifts together and all were later joined by other young men for a catered buffet. Why did she invite her son into this traditionally woman's domain? For two reasons. This shower marked the beginning of the marriage festivities and she wanted him to share in the memories. But more important, the bride's mother was seriously ill and not expected to live. Olga felt her future daughter-in-law needed her son's support at this traumatic time. Did she do the "right" thing? You decide. Following the wedding reception, she went into her son's old room to pick up a bit and found a note on his bed, addressed to her. It spoke of love and caring and gratitude for her sensitivity at this important time in their lives.

COOKIE-SAMPLER SHOWER

Especially nice for a morning coffee klatch shower, the Cookie-Sampler can be held almost any time of day. Ask each guest to prepare the dough from a favorite cookie recipe and bring it to the shower on cookie sheets, ready to be popped into the oven. Then simply sample each batch immediately after baking, along with a suitable beverage.

To tie in gifts with this theme, guests might give baking pans, cookie cutters or other kitchen items. Of course, the recipe for the cookie sampled should also be included with each gift.

Since cookie baking time is usually 8-12 minutes, there'll be just enough time for a fresh round of coffee, good conversation, praise for each cookie chef, and for taste buds to adjust.

This is a very social, easy-going shower and a good way for good friends to celebrate together. In fact, believe it or not, the one we heard about was held for the mother of the bride, without the bride or groom being present (though they can be). A group of Mom's friends and neighbors came together to celebrate HER emancipation . . . and all gifts and recipes went to the grateful couple.

A shower without the bride or groom? At first glance that may sound unbelievable, we agree. But when you think about it, it's a perfect way to lend support to the parents who are "losing" a son or daughter . . . or gaining more freedom for themselves.

Best of all, Mom was able to freeze the extra cookies . . . and they came in mighty handy for quick, informal entertaining during hectic pre-wedding days!

HANDY-ANDY/ HARDWARE-HANNAH SHOWER

Believe it or not, in some places the stag party and bachelor bash are phasing out. Instead, friends or family of the groom are throwing a Handy-Andy/Hardware-Hannah shower for him, or for the couple. Besides having a "masculine" flavor, it's also a tremendous source of practical gift giving.

Hardware stores are gold mines of gadgets and necessities. This one simplifies gift-giving like nothing else: scissors, batteries, nails, tacks, hammers, screw drivers, wrenches, ladders, kerosene lamps, brooms, picture hangers—the list is endless. Such items are a big investment for the couple, but barely noticeable when each guest brings one or two. These are the kinds of things the couple

won't think about until they're about to hang a picture . . .
oops! No hammer.

Your invitation can be on the humorous side, with a
cartoon of two inept handy-persons. You might even try
writing a four-line verse to get your point across. Not artis-
tic or poetic? That's O.K. Just see our INVITATION
GUIDE for a printer-ready sample. We've combined a cartoon AND a verse!

In our version, we've suggested that your guests bring
their gifts in the original bag, with the hardware motif on
the front. These can be tied with colored twine or rope. If
tied round and round several times, the couple has a nice
length for future use. Yes, when we get practical, we really
outdo ourselves!

Make your decorations as hardware-slanted as possible. A
table centerpiece using flowers, plumber's candles and pipe
joints (sprayed with gold or silver paint) can be created in
a jiffy. A flower arrangement encircled by assorted
wrenches or with hammers, wrenches and screwdrivers
placed right into the arrangement—are all eye-catching and
original. And, of course, there's the good old "plumber's
helper" Spray paint it a color, prop it up in the center of
the table, adorn it with flowers held in place with colorful
tacks, and in all probability, you'll be labeled VERY
original!

The gift opening area can be worked into this theme in
several ways. One big barrel would do the trick. Spiffy it up
with stain or paint and you've got a great container. Or you
can make a circle of wire fencing to corral the presents.

The activity for this theme is simply a "handy hints" session where each guest gives at least one suggestion. Everyone has at some time been faced with the need to fix something. Your guests will be in all age ranges and will represent many years of experience in fixing . . . or finding the easier way to do a variety of chores. This activity is a sharing of that expertise. Be sure to write down all hints (we suggest 3"x 5" cards), so the couple can refer to them in time of need. Another alternative is to ask each guest to write a handy hint beforehand and enclose it with the gift.

So, yes, this shower can replace the old stag party. And, yes, it makes for very practical gift giving. But best of all . . . you may never have to lend the couple one of YOUR prized tools!

 # APARTMENT/ CONDO POOL SHOWER

Jump right in . . . the water's fine! This shower's a natural for the active couple with friends who expect an action-packed time. Informality is the key. Guests come in their bathing suits, sports clothes, pool clogs, and bring along a towel or robe. The only inactive part of this event is gift-opening time. So reserve the pool area on your chosen date and have extra nose and ear plugs available.

To let your guests know this isn't just any shower, how about writing your invitation on an inflated plastic life preserver (the kind children use)? A permanent marking pen works best and will give you vivid colors Then deflate and insert it into a large envelope. Write a few catchy words on the envelope back, such as:

"Put a 'ring' around this date"

"Instructions, Blow, read . . . and BE THERE!"

"How about a real wet shower?"

Balloons will be your mainstay decoration. They'll give the pool a festive air and can also be used in your games and activities. So order plenty. If you plan far enough ahead, they can be personalized with the couple's names and wedding date. Order them through a novelty store or take a permanent marking pen and do-it-yourself . . . and if any are left intact, they can become keepsakes for the couple and guests.

Make your gifting special, too. Twist two colors of crepe paper streamers together (to resemble rope) and cordon off an area amid the deck chairs. Seat the couple in this spot at gift-opening time.

Place your refreshment table nearby and use general shower decorations (see our DECORATIONS GUIDE). Since most apartment/condo pools have kitchen facilities, you can plan hot or cold food. Just be sure to use plastic, paper or foam glasses, dinnerware and utensils, for safety reasons.

Now, get your whistle ready because here we go . . . on to the "Shower Olympics!" You've got people, water and b-a-l-l-o-o-n-s. So how about a:

1) WATER BALLOON FIGHT: Form teams, fill balloons with water and go to it!

2) BALLOON DISCUS THROW: Half-fill balloons with water. Use a net for the measure and set it higher as players are eliminated. No fair using two hands.

3) BALLOON RACE: Set up a "race track" on deck and line up the players. Guests kick their air-filled balloons down to the finish line . . . no hands allowed.

4) DISTANCE KICK: Measure who can kick an air-filled ballon the farthest.

5) WATER VOLLEYBALL: Use an air-filled balloon, of course!

These are just a few ideas, but almost any game can be adapted to the pool area. Remember the three-legged race, so popular at picnics? Just loosely bind people together at the ankles, two by two, and line them up in the shallow end. When the whistle blows, they race across the pool (width-wise), patting a balloon back and forth between the two. The first couple across wins.

Plan some "surprise times", too. Explain to guests that you'll blow a party horn (or ring a bell) at certain intervals. One blast means that if they're in the water . . . the first one OUT wins a prize. Two blasts if they're on deck . . . the first one IN gets the goodie. Do this occasionally at first, but at least once during your party, blast them in succession . . . In—out—in!

Make it a rule, please, that no one is allowed to throw, carry or push anyone else into the pool (tsk, tsk!). In fact, you might consider hiring a lifeguard for this occasion. The lifeguard can lay the ground rules and you'll rest easy, knowing you've created a safe, but fun atmosphere. Find a guard reference by calling any local community or school pool.

We doubt there'll be a dry body in the crowd as this event comes to a close, but just in case, award the escape artist a very special prize . . . a bouquet of colorful balloons!

Wrap up your party with a wine or juice cheer. Use plastic wine glasses and raise a toast to the showered couple:

"May you always 'pool' together!"

"May your wedded days be filled with joy, and that's no baloony!"

"May you always have time for popping balloons!"

Well, it's time to bid your guests good-bye . . . very wet but invigorated and happy. You can be sure they'll also be water-logged (ahem) with wonderful memories.

ANOTHER IDEA: From The Personal Touch, a Gift Store in York, Pennsylvania that offers ideas and designs—a shower for both the bride-and-groom-to-be, rather than just for the bride, is called . . . "A Drizzle!"

ROAST-THE-MANAGER SHOWER

When it's the boss's turn to say, "I do," the shower calls for a little executive ingenuity. After all, the boss is the boss! Chances are you'll want this shower to be something special. A "compliment" roast is a nice touch . . . just a few planned-ahead, pseudo-complimentary, funny remarks from each person, along with attention to menu, decorations and gift detail, will give you the makings of a shower-to-be-remembered (maybe at raise time!).

Over the lunch hour or immediately after the work day, seem to be the most favored times to hold this shower. But we've even heard of roasts held during extended coffee breaks.

Locations vary widely. You can stick to what's usually done in your area or consider these popular options: in the office conference room, over cocktails, at a nice restaurant for a sit-down dinner or buffet, in the company lunch room, with boxed lunches (see our "Co-Worker" shower theme).

In addition to your immediate department, guests may include the spouse-to-be, business friends, the manager's boss, other department heads, and even the president of the company. If you're planning a surprise shower, be sure to clear the date and time with the manager's secretary.

You can hold general decorations to a minimum, but you must do something absolutely crazy for the manager and his or her chair (see "No-Sweat" shower also). Here's what we mean: a Mickey Mouse beanie, a head band with antennae of sparkling stars or hearts, a wild ten-inch bow tie, a superman/woman cape, a grass skirt or a crown with office supplies attached (pens, pencils, rulers, or whatever applies). Decorate the chair-of-honor with crepe paper or foil streamers and colorful balloons. If you want to do a bit more, try a personalized fun poster (see our DECORATIONS GUIDE for both).

As you plan your roast "digs," plot some fun gifts you can present to the manager after each one. Your remarks need to be personal, so we can't help you there, but these gift ideas may spark your thinking: a T-shirt that says, "Who's boss now?", a mock paper ladder—for a quick getaway, a kerosene lamp—for light when the electricity bill hasn't been paid.

In addition to these fun gifts, one large present from the whole department seems to be the most popular solution. Season tickets to an event the couple enjoys, a romantic "dinner-for-two" gift certificate, and a one-time general house cleaning service are some unusual gift ideas. A briefcase or luggage, umbrella, personalized appointment book or brass business card holder are more common, but nevertheless, much appreciated.

Well, we've had our digs and some good fun besides. Its only fair now that we give the manager the opportunity to respond or to extend thanks to the group. It's a chance for us, also, to get a bit more serious and extend our sincere best wishes and happy marriage salutations. In other words ... after the monkey business ... it's back to business as usual!

BE-MY-VALENTINE SHOWER

What can be more romantic than a Valentine's Day wedding? You can take full advantage of this ready-made theme and play it to the hilt. There'll be no trouble finding decorations for this natural couples or mixed singles shower. If you stress the romantic, the sentimental and love, love, love—you'll have cupid tripping over arrows in mid-air!

Go all out with a red, pink and white color scheme and lots of romantic decorations. Red foil hearts and white paper wedding bells, red, white and pink crepe paper streamers, silver, heart-shaped balloons, and pink or silver cupids will all give your space the look you want.

Carry your decorations over to the refreshment table, too. A red floral centerpiece on a white tablecloth makes an attractive focal point. Dress it up with pink and white candles and you'll have a perfect set-up for dimming the lights! And how about gifting each guest with a red carnation . . . the symbol of love? Present it in the Cascade Napkin Fold to enhance your table even more (see our ACTIVITIES GUIDE).

Give your foods romantic names, too. Beverages can be "love potions," dinner rolls can be shaped into "love knots," and a casserole might be the "love pot." Consider cherry pie or a heart-shaped cake for dessert . . . better known as "sweetie pie" and "heart's desire," respectively. Make small labels and tape them to each food container. Write them in calligraphy, a most romantic script . . . red ink on white paper, of course.

To keep everyone in a love-ly spirit, gather up as many romantic ballad records or cassette tapes as possible. Now who wouldn't succumb to "My Funny Valentine" or "Love

Makes the World Go 'Round?'' Lilting background music can add a very special touch. But if you really want to get mellow, hire a harpist or piano player to softly serenade your guests and the honored couple.

Now how about your invitation? We couldn't find a specific Valentine shower invitation, but you may be able to in your area. Of course, you could purchase a package of children's Valentine cards, so popular at that time of year. All you'd have to do is write your invitation on the reverse side. But if you prefer a tailor-made invitation for a valentine wedding shower, we think a short verse would be nice. How does this sound?

> Cupid brought them together
> And soon they'll be one.
> Come to this Valentine shower
> And join in the fun!

If you like the idea, just turn to our INVITATIONS GUIDE for a printer-ready copy. Choose a pink paper and have it printed in red ink. Then, after printing, add a little pizzazz to the envelope with red foil hearts of different sizes. Any drug or gift store carries the self-adhesive kind.

Well, what more can we say? Every shower celebrates a love story . . . and this theme can make your shower a real labor of love!

ANOTHER IDEA: If you like this theme, but you're not showering a Valentine wedding couple, why not do as Fran Maloney of Fridley, Minnesota suggests? Simply change it to a "Something-To-Go-With-Love" shower.

ANOTHER IDEA: Fran also sent us a good favor idea she used with a large guest list. She made small, heart-shaped pillows, trimmed with lace and sewed two silver rings in the center of each. They were numbered on the back and pinned to guests as they arrived. Several nice door prizes were awarded as matching numbers were drawn.

MEET-THE-RELATIVES SHOWER

This event is actually more than a shower. It's a unique opportunity to foster a good relationship between the two families who'll quite possibly be seeing a lot of each other in the future. Many times they're practically strangers, and for this reason we suggest everyone be invited—mothers, fathers, sisters, brothers, aunts, uncles and cousins of each immediate family.

So we'll start right off with a name tag or favor that states the guest's name AND relationship to the bride or groom. Mary McGinn of Roseville, Minnesota, sent us directions for making "Pillow-Puff"—a small rectangle of satin, edged with lace and filled with a "puff" of nylon batting. Then press a white address label to the front and you have a very pretty name tag (see our FAVORS GUIDE). The point is for everyone to get to know everyone else a little better and this is a good beginning.

Another way to encourage intermingling is to plan a sit-down dinner or a buffet with enough table groupings to seat everyone. Then use place cards to position one of his relatives next to one of hers, and on around until everyone has a place next to a member of the "other" family. This tactic, along with the name tag, can get the conversation ball rolling very nicely.

Now that you've got people in a position to talk to each other, what can they talk ABOUT? Well, let's see . . . what's the one thing they all have in common? You're right! The wedding couple. So, back to name tags. After these have been distributed, people will be trying to communicate with each other . . . in other words, it's liable to be strained.

"So, you're 'her' aunt Bea? I've heard so much about you!"

"I sure am. Uh-huh. Yes siree."

Let's take them out of their misery. Now this calls for lots of special bait . . . hung on the walls and from lampshades, on tables and windowsills . . . anywhere. As you can see, we're not going to be subtle.

The bait, of course, is anything graphic that has to do with the couple: scrap books, blown up baby picture posters, photos, home movies, awards, trophies, letters of recognition, etc. You should have quite a collection of items dating back to the birth of the two babes.

Here's how we suggest you do it. Alert family members at least two months ahead so they'll have time to gather these treasures of the past. Of course, you can do this by telephone, but ShowerWise came up with a smashing invitation we think is perfect. It contains just three lines of verse with a short explanation (see our INVITATIONS GUIDE). It should bring you what you need.

At shower time, place the collection you've harvested in obvious places. If you've been able to obtain home movies, run these continuously (and off to the side), so those who are interested may watch whenever they like.

The highlight of this shower is the presentation of a special gift to the couple. Ask both families for a copy of their family tree. An artist or calligrapher can make these look very professional. Place them side by side in an elegant frame and gift wrap. We suggest that you consider eliminating the usual custom of gift-giving. Because our intent in this shower is to cement relations, not to start a gifting competition, the framed family trees serve as a lasting memento from both families.

This shower is one that lends support to the couple and attempts to unite, not only two people, but two families as well. Make it work for you and the old saying, "To know you is to love you," will become a reality.

THE ELEGANT SHOWER

Strictly elegant, from the chic invitation to the favor each guest takes home, this shower has flair. No expense is spared to add the extra, special touches that set the mood. The use of satin decorations instead of paper, lavish baskets and garlands of fresh flowers, and an imported champagne toast are just a few of the embellishments. Yes, it's lavish ... but strictly in good taste.

A gracious home, the country club setting, a fine supper club or patio restaurant are all likely locations. Plan a leisurely luncheon or sit-down dinner to show off this shower to its best advantage.

Personalize your invitation by hiring a balloon-a-gram service to deliver a dozen silver and gold balloons to each guest, with a formal, printed invitation attached. These companies will also compose a persuasive jingle for you. This can be very dramatic, but only if the verse is in good taste. A bouquet of fresh flowers can also create the desired effect.

If you really want to impress the guest of honor, arrange to have her picked up by limousine. If you want to impress your guests, too, . . . send the car 'round for all of them. Did we say elegant or didn't we?

Collaborate closely with the maitre d' for an elaborate service. A champagne fountain or shower-type sculpture (watering can, umbrella, wedding bells) make eye-catching centerpieces. A small music box favor that plays a romantic melody can also double as a distinctive place card. Or use miniature baskets of silk flowers in the same way.

Chances are that all gifts will be brought to the shower splendidly adorned. Should your gift-opening area be anything less? Create an extra special temporary home for these beauties with the use of satin props and fresh flower garlands.

Good conversation is the activity here, so provide the opportunity for leisurely chatting betweeen the bride, family members and guests. Soft background music, either live or piped in, can help to fashion an effective atmosphere. Allow enough time for this most pleasant interaction and for your guests to "take in" the beautiful setting you've created.

Top off your party with a sparkling toast, served in "Flute" champagne glasses, so popular years ago and making a comeback, perhaps because of their bubble-saving design. Encourage your guests to take part by expressing their warm thoughts and well wishes.

It's too bad this day will soon be over. Then all we'll have left is the magnificent memory. But wait! Not so fast. Why don't we record this lovely time on film? A video tape or an album of still photographs is a lasting keepsake for the bride . . . of this special day she was honored . . . the splendid way in which she was honored . . . and the person who honored her . . . YOU!

DOLLAR-DISCO-DANCE SHOWER

What do you give the couple who'll be off to another state immediately following the ceremony? Chances are you'll hesitate to burden them with heavy crockery, blankets or dinnerware. Our solution? Something light, extremely useful, and green ... MONEY! Although the gifting of money at a shower may not be considered "good taste" in some parts of the country, when everyone is having such a good time, it seems to soften the mercenary aspect. This is great fun when lots of people take part and solves the gift problem beautifully.

Since you're going for large numbers, invite relatives, friends, business associates, and their families. Children love taking part in these affairs and feel very special when invited.

If you live in a small town, your invitation can be extended through an announcement in the local weekly newspaper, or by word-of-mouth. In a larger city, you can form "calling teams"—each person calls five to ten families. Of course, in either case, you may choose to send out formal invitations.

You'll need a dance floor and seating area large enough to accommodate the group. VFW halls, country clubs, golf clubs, and large meeting rooms in motels and hotels would all be good choices.

Pick an evening that most people will be available. We suggest Friday or Saturday, after dinnertime. Then all you'll have to furnish are snacks: peanuts, pretzels, popcorn, potato chips, punch and a cash bar.

When you're making rental arrangements, find out what the agent can supply. Most places have at least some appropriate decorations, lighting and a microphone. Then fill in where you need to. Hire a small dance band with a leader who will also emcee. To keep costs down, you can use records, cassettes or a juke box, but we like to economize somewhere else. There's just something about LIVE music!

You'll find a table centerpiece suggestion in our DECOR-ATIONS GUIDE that would be perfect for this shower called "Mirrored Reflection." A printed card to inform guests of the dollar dance procedure can be propped up in this centerpiece.

Enough background "music" . . . let's get on with the dance! We suggest you plan five "cash" dances. Four of them will be $1 dances and one will cost $5 (set your own prices). Most dances will be free. Your M.C. should plan two $1 dances in the beginning of the evening and two nearer the end. The $5 dance should start in about the middle of the evening, when late-comers have arrived and early-goers are still present. These dances should be lively and as long as possible. End the music when all of the guests who wanted to, have danced with the couple.

All dances should be announced with a drum roll and great fanfare. You'll need several people to help add to the excitement by encouraging 'buyers' to form two lines, one to dance with HER and the other to dance with HIM. They'll also act as "cashiers," collecting the dollars in a hat and allowing about 30 to 60 seconds per dance. Then . . . and here's the surprise . . . when the music suddenly stops, the two people who are dancing with the bride and groom win a prize! Your prizes can be bought or donated, but they should be displayed throughout the evening. Some sugges-tions are: photo album, plant, floral arrangement, book-ends, magazine rack, two movie tickets, etc. Of course, the most coveted prizes are won during the $5 dance.

Well, to be sure, the engaged couple will never forget this night . . . and the generosity of everyone. They'll be off to their new home in a new state with very fond memories of all those good dancers they left behind!

ANOTHER IDEA: Norma Flora of Commack, New York sent us an easy favor idea that would work well for a large group. Just fill a small square of netting with colored rice and tie it all up with a pretty white ribbon.

TIE-A-QUILT SHOWER

For the sentimental among you, this shower can be given for the bride-to-be in a church circle, service group, or any group that meets regularly (bridge, bowling, etc.). The idea is to give the honored guest a tangible, lasting, from-the-heart gift. And that it is, as each member makes a quilt square at home and helps complete the quilt at the shower, amid good cheer and good friends.

We must say, this was one of the most meaningful showers we've attended and we did actually help make a memory quilt. But the idea is too good; there's no reason why it can't be used to create other treasures. How about a wall hanging instead? Just do it up with mini-squares. And if you're not into stitchery, how about original, hand-drawn squares, using colorful textile markers for either version?

Each square is stitched or drawn with a symbol or message. They're accompanied by an album of short notes explaining the significance of each piece, and the best wishes and signature of the giver. During the shower, the quilt is tied and hemmed over good conversation. When it's completed, each person reads her own contribution from the album.

It's important to choose an overall theme for the squares, such as state flowers, geometric figures, old quilt patterns, or motifs that are meaningful in the wedding couple's life. We chose, 'marriage advice.' This is always a good subject, but your own group should be in on this part of the planning.

We were pleased with our combination of humor and sensitivity. On one square Sue Goldade of Bloomington, Minnesota, had two bears cuddled under a quilt. The album inscription was, "To save energy AND a marriage—cuddle!" Ours portrayed a pineapple, an old symbol of southern hospitality. The wish was that, "each one would be hospitable to change and growth in the other."

So, here you have a ready-made shower activity. About one month before the chosen date, invite members to take part. At this time, distribute instructions for the quilt squares and agree on the type of stitchery everyone should use (applique, cross stitching, embroidery, etc.). Instructions should include the size, color scheme and type of fabric for the squares. A set fee is collected for the batting and backing material. Finished squares are sent to one person who will sew them together with edging strips (stitched squares may be alternated with squares of solid-colored fabric, also). You should set a deadline for completion.

About half an hour before shower time, members meet to make final preparations. The backing layer is stretched over the quilting frame. Batting is placed over it and the top layer (the sewn together squares) is laid over that. A quick basting stitch is taken (all around) to hold the layers together.

If your secret has been well kept, the bride-to-be will be truly surprised when she arrives. Then, all members, along with the bride, tie the quilt and finish the edges as your quilt party progresses. No other arrangements need be made for this shower, except provision for some refreshment. Our meetings are always potluck, and we just carried this through. Since you're all in this together, make it a group decision.

So put your camera on automatic, gather 'round the handsome quilt and snap several group photos. Give one to each member, and to the bride as a lasting memento.

This shower gives, gives, gives . . . warm feelings . . . warm memories . . . AND a warm bed!

ANOTHER IDEA: This theme can connect the couple with distant relatives or those who won't be attending the celebration. In this case, send material, along with the instructions. Did Haberman of New Brighton, Minnesota was asked to make a quilt square for her great-niece who lived several states away. She enjoyed being included in the plans for this lasting gift.

ANOTHER IDEA: Lee Campbell of Penn Wynne, Pennsylvania, suggests supplying each guest with a 3"x 3" square of pellon (found in fabric stores) and a marking pen. Ask them to print the one word they think is most important in a marriage. Then glue all squares together for an instant wall hanging gift.

 # OFFICE CO-WORKER SHOWER

What could be easier than a shower for one of your co-workers? If you think of it as a glorified coffee break, everything can be planned and executed in less time than it takes to write a memo. Well, maybe that's a slight exaggeration, but catered box lunches, simple decorations and one big gift from the group makes this shower E-A-S-Y!

Almost any deli has a box lunch containing a sandwich, salad or slaw, pickles, potato chips and cookies. Call in your order the day before and it will be ready and waiting (maybe even delivered) at the appointed time. However, if your co-workers have the "before pay-day jitters," perhaps you'll opt for a "bring-your-own-bag" lunch. Just be sure someone is appointed to bring an extra bag (or order an extra box) for the guest-of-honor.

You probably already know the best place in your area to hold this type of shower, but we'll mention a few places we've heard of that you might not have considered. Do you have a conference room available? How about a corner of your company lunch room? Weather permitting, a nearby park area with picnic benches would also be nice. In California, beach showers are "in".

Many co-worker showers are also held in restaurants where you'll either order from the menu, or arrange a group menu beforehand. Don't rule out a corner of your company cafeteria either. It's more public, yes, but for some reason, when someone's about to be married, they love the attention. Besides, it won't hurt your company image to be known as a friendly and caring department.

Held indoors or out, your "picnic" should be a celebration. So be sure to bring along lots of balloons and streamers. Look through our DECORATIONS GUIDE for more ideas you can use.

But wait—while you're back there, also see our GIFT GUIDE if your co-workers prefer to give their own individual gifts. A lot depends on the area of the country, but most often we've see the big group gift win out. You can make it special by tying the wrapping in with your department. For instance, Computer department—printout paper; Finance department—columnar paper; Mail room—"Air Mail, Fragile, First Class," etc., rubber stamped all over colorful paper; Graphics Department—congratulatory messages and illustrations keylined on solid white.

Now about that memo—make it your invitation! Use "Memo" or "From the desk of . . ." notepaper. Simply type it up like this:
"SUBJECT: Very Important Occasion—This takes precedence over all other letters, files, reports, meetings, etc., etc., etc."

You'll find a printer-ready copy in our INVITATIONS GUIDE if you'd rather use that. Add your own information using a black, thin-lined marker. Then have it printed or copy it on the office copy machine, and pass it around.

As you can see, this shower lends itself to several possibilities. Whether you decide to bag it, cater it, dine in or picnic out, you'll surely add to the happy memories of one of your co-workers.

SHARE-A-MENU SHOWER

How'd you like to have two week's worth of breakfasts, lunches and dinners planned in advance? Sound good? Well it surely will to the new bride and groom, too. We've taken the popular "recipe" shower one step further. Instead of bringing their favorite recipe, guests donate their most successful menu, complete to the last detail.

Goblet or wine glass? Place mats or table cloth? Guests describe how they do it ... with all recipes for the entire meal included. The intended couple benefits because they'll end up with the cream of the crop. And guests go home with as many new recipes as they care to jot down. Since many more men are becoming adept in the kitchen and at the barbecue grill, don't overlook this one for a couples shower.

Your invitation should give specific instructions so that guests understand they will each compile their own menu booklet. A BOOKLET?!!! Yes, a booklet, made with 3"x 5" index cards with two punch holes along the top.

The first card lists the menu—appetizer, main course, side dish, salad, dessert—along with a suitable greeting:

O   **FOR SUE & BOB**   O
Our best for two of the very best!
MENU
Golden Dip
Baked Ham California
Red Apple Rings
Golden Gate Salad
Wine
Lemon Tarts
From Aunt Rose & Uncle George.

Subsequent cards contain the recipes for each dish. Special touches are explained on cards following the recipes. After the set is assembled, a pretty, colored ribbon can be looped through the holes, tied ... and there you have it ... a booklet! ... or, more accurately, a booklet from each of your guests. Then you supply a recipe box and the couple has a veritable "treasure" chest!

Include at least six index cards with your invitation. Ask guests to make their menu gift as unique as possible. They can decorate with markers, photos, magazine pictures, fabric, etc. Just noting the name of the showered person or couple, the date and the occasion makes the cards much more personal. And be sure to indicate that they'll have an opportunity to copy any recipes they'd like for their own collection. The more recipe cards you make available at your shower, the fewer games and activities you'll need to plan.

Now, how about a keepsake for each of your guests for doing such a good job? Janis Farrington of the Table Top Shoppe in Lombard, Illinois sent us a favor suggestion we thought would be a nice addition to this shower. Her idea? Fill a heart or bell-shaped cookie cutter with candy or nuts. Then tie the whole package together with netting and a pretty bow.

Anyone who loves to cook, loves to swap recipes. And that's what this shower is . . . a glorified swap session.

ANOTHER IDEA: Guests bring a recipe inserted into the container in which it will be cooked or frozen. An herb or spice needed in preparation may also be added.

ANOTHER IDEA: Plan a dessert tasting/recipe swapping shower.

SURPRISE - FRIENDSHIP SHOWER

This shower takes some pre-arranging, but we promise, it's one that will be remembered long after the wedding fanfare. It was held in Michigan for Jessica Fallon, the person who told us about it. She's been married for fifteen years and still has fond memories.

If good friends and relatives are scattered around the country and are coming in for the wedding, invite them in town a few days early for a shower-to-be-remembered. This must be a surprise, so the wedding couple should merely be told these guests will try to attend the wedding. As you can see, this shower is held as close as possible to the wedding date.

Chances are everyone will have a lot of catching up to do, but you may have time for one activity. Lucy Oxberry of San Diego, California suggests a drawing of each guest done with a bright lamp beam. Then a guessing of which silhouette belongs to each guest brings a small prize to the winner.

To spark recollections, encourage guests to bring along photos from the 'old days', yearbooks, pennants, and other paraphernalia from when the group was together. Dig out any remembrances that would be appropriate. You don't actually NEED these, but they'll add just the right flavor.

While you're at it, you might ask your guests to gift the couple with an item their adopted state is known for: From Minnesota—wild rice and casserole dish; from Washington —apples and fruit bowl; from California—wine and wine glasses. On the other hand, being surrounded by far-flung friends can be gift enough.

A nice menu touch is to plan a home town food that guests have likely been hankering for. Is there a favorite pizza the gang used to order when they got together? How about Mom's fried chicken? Whatever you choose . . . make sure there's plenty of the favorite to go around two or three times!

After your guests have made this giant effort to be present, a couple of poignant favors would be a nice show of appreciation. Two ideas we like will give them a remembrance of the occasion and a bit of help to stay in touch in the future.

First . . . take plenty of instant pictures. Be sure each guest is "snapped" with the couple. Then pose the group as a whole and take as many shots as necessary to give each guest one for the road.

Second . . . purchase a small address book for each guest. Either enter all names, addresses and phone numbers in it, or have the guests themselves do it. Be sure to include the current addresses of those who weren't able to attend.

Whether guests pay their own fares, or the hostess or parents of the couple choose to do the honors, this shower is like a fairy tale come true.

CALORIE- COUNTER SHOWER

Here's a dieter's dream! Guests know beforehand there'll be no frou-frou desserts, extra calories or pounds . . . and no temptation! It's perfect for people who belong to the dieter groups springing up around the country. Since dieting is so popular, you'll find food and gifts a cinch. There's plenty on the market in drug stores, gift shops and special diet sections in grocery stores.

If you do belong to a dieter's group, read over our "No-Sweat" theme. This shower can be held in much the same way, using your meeting location instead of a sports room. Otherwise, arrange to gather at someone's home afterwards. One of the health food restaurants is another possibility.

Of course, any friend or relative may be invited, but this shower is especially for the dieter's support group that wants to shower one of their own. The menu is simple fare. In fact, since diets differ, you may want to suggest that each member bring his or her own diet food or snack.

Any general wedding shower decorations are fine, but

incorporating diet slogans can add a personal touch. Some we've seen are:

"Marriage is like dieting—Forever!"

"Two can live as cheaply as one—but only while dieting!"

"Happiness is being a dieter and marrying one!"

"Live on Love . . . NOT on calories!"

These can be made into across-the-chest banners (a la Miss America). Use a marking pen on 3″wide, colored strips of paper, about two yards in length. A classier version can be made with textile pen on ribbon. Both can be secured in the back with two paper clips or pins. It's a way to make your guests part of the decorations and a good technique when you're short on time or space.

As in the "No-Sweat" theme, you probably won't have time for games or activities. However, if you've decided to hold the shower in a home, you may want to plan a recipe exchange, since you'll have more time. This activity, geared to diet recipes, should be a welcomed addition.

We've seen so many dieter gimmicks in our scouting around, we know favors for your guests can be easily found. Dieter slogans decorate refrigerator magnets, aprons, T-shirts, plaques, plates, pins, etc. If you're handy, you can create mementos by printing the slogans on 2″x 2″ cardboard or painting them on wood (for a more lasting version) and attaching a magnetic square to the back. The self-adhesive magnets can be found in most drug or craft stores.

These diet reminders can either shout or subtly tell their messages from refrigerators, auto dash boards, picture frames ... or wherever metal can meet metal.

Well, there you have it ... and we didn't say "gooey dessert" once!

HOLLYWOOD STARS SHOWER

Lights! Camera! Action! Here's a shower you can have lots of fun with. Set it up to resemble a Hollywood premiere. From the moment you greet your guests with a mock microphone, to the time they leave with their "Oscars," they'll feel they've really been to a celebrity opening.

Now there's a lot to this shower so you really have to pay attention. But if you're tired of doing the same old thing, and you have friends who enjoy "hamming" it up, you could receive an Academy Award for your efforts!

Your invitation should be as intriguing as possible. We suggest you pattern it after a theater program, naming your guests as the "star-studded cast." Ask them to be prepared to mimic the mannerisms and speech of a famous star (Bette Davis, Clark Gable, Bette Midler, Zsa Zsa Gabor, Burt Reynolds, Humphrey Bogart, etc.). Be sure to tell them to come and collect their Oscars!

You'll need to gather or make as many theater and movie props as possible: spot lights, marquee lights, film frames, photos of movie stars, Take-Boards, long cigarette holders, director's chairs, a Call-Board, etc. Your props, together with anything that glitters (foil, tinsel, sequined material), should be combined to create your "set." Then if you have, or can beg, borrow, steal or rent a home video camera and recorder, you'll be all set for a great production.

The bride and groom should be the first to arrive. Give them choice seats (decorated director's chairs, of course) so they can watch and contribute to the "filming." Supply them with sunglasses, a cheerleader megaphone and a pair of berets.

Try to arrange it so that most of your guests arrive at the same time. Start the camera rolling as you usher them in, one couple at a time, just as you've seen TV M.C.'s do at preview showings and premieres. With microphone, or a mock microphone if the real one is in the camera, welcome each couple with a few remarks. Speak to them as the people they've chosen to imitate, but also to them as they really are. Go for a blend of fantasy and reality. For instance, you might say, "Here they are folks, that ravishing couple from Baker Street in Indiana (real), Burt Reynolds and Bette Midler (fantasy). He's the proud father of the bride (real). I believe Bette is his sixth wife and owner of her own investment firm (fantasy). Hello, you two—do you have a few words of advice for the happy couple?" Greet other guests in the same "Hollywood" style, leading them to the wedding couple for an exchange of "advice" and impromptu remarks. Try to get all reactions on camera, both from the people speaking and the ones who've already been welcomed and are now watching.

Once inside, and after the first flow of greetings and conversation, bring on the fresh plaster of Paris. Yes, we said plaster. This should be poured in a container about twenty-four inches square. Have you heard of Graumann's Chinese Restaurant? That's the place where the prints of the stars are embedded forever in cement. Well, we'll call this your mini Graumann's. Each guest is invited to leave a thumb print along with their name and by so doing, receives an "Oscar" (made of children's Play-Doh™)for an outstanding performance as a mother, father, friend, etc. The plaster plaque becomes a wall hanging for the couple so be sure to insert a hanger in back before it drys.

Are you still rolling the camera? Fine! For refreshments, appetizers and cocktails should do nicely. Encourage your guests to stay in "character" throughout the evening. This adds to the fun.

Got your cue cards ready? Good, because now it's gift time. As the couple opens each gift, they must only say what has been written on the cards you hold up. Some comments might be, "Should this be used in the morning or at night?" and "Boy, what we can do with this" and "Now here's something we can take to bed with us!" and on and on. Know your guests and cue accordingly.

Now it's time to run the film. Settle your guests with bowls of popcorn (what else?) and play back the film of the evening's antics.

As irreverent as this shower may seem, the spoofs are all in good fun. If you think the wedding couple and your guests can make it work, then go to it . . . and on with the show!

CO-HOSTESS SHOWER

Here's a shower idea that's becoming popular around the country. It's for people who lead busy lives and don't have the time needed to host a shower by themselves. Because it's not only enjoyable, but divides the work and expenses, the guest list can be substantial. Planning as a team can be more fun too. No one person has to do it all and everyone can participate at the level they'd like.

Liz Joseph of Hopkins, Minnesota shared this midwestern version of the idea with us: The shower is usually held in a restaurant, over luncheon. After the location and menu have been chosen, calculate the donation each person must make. Be aware of all expenses so no one will be left with more than her share. Invite the bride, her mother, the groom's mother and all siblings, gratis. Other items, such as gift wrap, flowers, special entertainment, etc., should be in the budget from the planning stage. Then figure the contribution each guest should make in order for the event to break even. For example, if the luncheon is $10.00 per plate, the gift contribution $12.50 and incidental items $2.50 per person, ask for $25.00. Guests have the option of sending a check for gift only if they can't attend. And, of course, if several people wish to donate beyond that—say to supply live background music—that's just dandy.

Based on the amount of money you've collected, several lovely gifts can be purchased, wrapped and delivered. Or you can opt for a single, more "important" offering.

Since your setting will already be quite pleasant, you need only add the finishing touches to the table(s). Fresh flowers and fun-wrapped, smaller gifts can be used as attractive centerpieces. Then as the bride-to-be opens each gift, she can interact with guests at that particular table, or that section of a larger table.

Extend your invitation via the phone or the mails. If phoning, "round-robin" your calls from a list supplied by the couple's parents. Each person reaches five to ten potential guests, explaining the event, time, place and cost. Many times you'll receive an acceptance on the spot. By written invitation, the same information is given, along with the name and phone number of your R.S.V.P. person.

This shower is a time-saver for those who are busy with job, family and other activities. It's also a reaching out of many friends to honor the bride, and because of that, creates a special feeling among all who attend.

ANOTHER IDEA: From the Marble Corner Gift Store in Mattoon, Illinois—"A champagne (or sparkling wine) brunch has been very successful for the past couple of years. No games. It gives guests a chance to visit and is a delightful noontime shower."

NO-SWEAT SHOWER

Are you a fitness-freak? Chances are, one of your class or team mates will be tying the knot sooner or later. No Sweat! Another example of bringing the shower to the group instead of the other way around, it's a nifty idea for after a class session or game. Informal, from its locker room location to the fruit drink you can serve, it's just absolutely no sweat for anyone.

The best part, of course, is this shower's informality. No one has to dress up or even clean house. And whether it's a group effort, or the planning of one or two people, no extensive preparations must be made.

The surprise element is crucial here and becomes part of the activity—decorating the bride's (or groom's) chair, mat or space. Here's how it works. When the class session or game is over, gather 'round the honored guest and shout, "surprise!" Then, blindfold and lead her to the party area amid the usual chatter. Bring out the crepe paper streamers, balloons, bells and any other noisy props that will pique her curiosity and keep her guessing.

Take two or three minutes to decorate a sitting space where she'll open her gifts. Just fasten balloons to the back of her chair and string bows, plastic flowers, string confetti or crepe paper streamers from it to reach down to the floor.

While some of the guests are doing the decorating, the others are setting out refreshments. To keep it simple, serve a fruit drink and oatmeal-raisin cookies. If you want to get more elaborate, we suggest a yogurt dip with fresh vegetables.

While all of these preparations are in the works, choose one of two strategies: either keep the chatter going or be absolutely quiet, so all that can be heard is the noise of the props.

Then, off comes the blindfold to another chorus of, "surprise!" ... and on with the party. Gift opening and snacking are done simultaneously.

Most often, invitations won't be necessary, especially when the whole group hosts the affair. But if one or two people take charge, consider an invitation card pinned to a clever T-shirt. We found some that would be great ... wedding bells, two entwined hearts, and some with appropriate verse. Visit your local T-shirt shop to see what's available. Remind guests to bring them along to the shower. They can be slipped on while the bride is blindfolded. Another clever idea is to make pullover vests out of white plastic garbage bags (see our DECORATIONS GUIDE). It's called, "decorating" your guests when you can't easily decorate your surroundings!

If you'd like to do a little extra something, Zallas Card and Gift Shop in Saugus, Massachusetts tells us one of their best selling wedding shower favors is a dry potpourri packet.

This theme may well have been sub-titled, "The One-Hour Shower" because, from start to finish, that's about how long it should take ... and that's part of its charm. Most classes and some games are held Monday through Thursday. People are anxious to get home, showered, and into bed in preparation for the next work day. They're most willing to spend an extra hour for such an occasion, but not much more. So keep it short, lively and festive!

ROMANTIC NOVEL SHOWER

"He took her in his arms, pressed her close to him and . . . . !" How's that for openers? The popularity of the romantic novel makes this a real fantasy shower. It's especially suited to a couple with dramatic flair. If your group is part of the romantic novel cult, you can let your imagination run wild.

Your decorations should shout, "romance, romance, romance!" Some novel-like setting could be: a magnolia garden; a photographer's studio; a Kentucky horse farm. The trick is to choose a popular novel and to recreate its setting. You may have to hunt up fake grass, magnolia blossoms, or a race track, but don't despair. If you're near a retail or theater supply house, you'll be able to buy or rent almost any item used to stage a play or a sale. Try bookstores, too. Many times, display posters are discarded for lack of room. Other ideas can be found in our UNUSUAL LOCATIONS GUIDE.

The activity for this shower focuses around gift opening. So once you have your novel, read through it and select as many juicy parts as there will be gifts.

At gift time, read one scene at a time, using the wedding couple's names in place of the book's characters. The couple, themselves, must act out what you say and they must read ONLY the "speaking parts" or dialogue. There's ALWAYS a romantic triangle in such stories, so one or two guests can help out.

You'll probably need several "rehearsals" because the guests are also the "directors." Anyone can give the couple ideas for trying the scene another way. Show the couple they've got the scene just right by a round of applause.

When this happens, one gift can be opened. Repeat until all scenes have been played and all gifts have been opened.

Be sure to record this on audio or video tape. It can be played back over refreshments or during the meal. Then, of course, it's given to the couple as a memento.

Once you've decided on your general atmosphere decorations, you can zero in on specifics. For the refreshment table, the romantic novel paperback you've chosen can stand upright at each place setting, naming each guest as its author. These become place cards and take-home favors. They also serve as the "script" for your gift-opening activity.

Try to do something spectacular for the gift-opening area. One idea is to make a very large replica of the paperback cover using a folding screen. Stand it up to become an enclosure for gifts and a backdrop for your "scenes" (see our DECORATIONS GUIDE).

Your invitation can be made to look like the cover of the paperback edition of the novel you've chosen, too. In addition to date, time, place, etc., tell your guests you plan to bring the novel to life at the shower, and to come prepared to help "direct" the action.

This shower is really not for the faint-hearted. It's far-out. It's fantasy. And it's worth every bit the extra effort for those determined to do something different!

 # WOK-ON-THE-WILD-SIDE SHOWER

Here's a surprising variation of the potluck dinner. While guests don't bring the food, they do prepare and cook it ... with a little help from a wok and you. It's a great idea for a couples or mixed singles shower. Something zany happens to people who cook together and you won't have to worry about any lulls in conversation. Sipping and munching while the feast is being prepared is a must.

This shower contains two "activities" which are central to the theme. The first activity is to get your guests busy making their own aprons from white plastic garbage bags (see pattern directions in our DECORATIONS GUIDE). Supply each person with a bright-colored, permanent marking pen. Instruct them to print a message on their apron, such as: "I wok-ed on the wild side at Joan and Jim's Wedding Shower." Or each apron could have one word on it. When the guests line up (before or after the meal), the aprons reveal the place of a hidden gift or a congratulatory/best wishes message for the showered couple. Or, guests can write their own "marriage advice" to the couple. And if they pen their own name in the upper left corner, the apron also serves as a name tag.

Now you're ready for the second activity, which has guests preparing the meal, a stir-fry dinner. Our menu suggestion is shrimp and/or chicken with vegetables. All the jobs—cleaning, peeling, chopping—are easy to do. Naturally, you'll want to supervise because this may be a new experience for some of your guests, but that's part of the fun. If you organize "work areas" beforehand, people will feel comfortably close, but not on top of each other. Then all you'll need to add are fortune cookies and jasmine tea ... perhaps a bit of Oriental mood music in the background ... and you have the makings of a delightful and satisfying buffet or sit-down meal.

If this shower appeals to you, be sure to visit a gift shop that sells Oriental items while you're still in the planning stage. We did, and found a gold mine of ideas: lanterns and Tientsin kites (for decorations), small origami containers (nut cups), an obi sash and a bamboo straw mat (table runners or wall hanging), brocaded silk pillow cases (placemats), ornate chopsticks (nice touch), tiny jewelry boxes (favor/place card), and decorated slippers (remember the Oriental custom of removing shoes and donning slippers?). But, the best idea we found was the inspiration for our invitation—FANS! Select a size that will slip into a large #10 business envelope, open the fan, print your invitation on it, fold it again, and mail. Now, wouldn't an invitation like that make you sit up and take notice?

All in all, this shower combines many of the ingredients you've asked for. It's a good one for couples or mixed singles. It gives people something to DO. It helps conversation flow. But most of all, it creates a warm, happy memory for all.

 # GIFT-THEME GALLERY

In some parts of the country, showers have a set pattern that would be very difficult to break. They worked just fine in the past and they'll work just as well in the future. After all, why argue with success? And yet . . . you'd like the next shower you hold to be just a bit different. Nothing wild, mind you. Just something that might leave people with the feeling that you are so-o-o clever.

Well, here's the secret. Do everything else as you've always done, or as custom dictates. Type of food, decorations, invitation, etc., can all stay within the pattern. Only now, you'll put the emphasis on the gift-giving portion of your shower. Use our gallery of gift-theme ideas when you already know the main shower plan. They're a way of adding a little extra something to the occasion, without too much change.

WEDDING REGISTRY SHOWER

Ever been to a shower where one gift was duplicated, two—even three times? This one absolutely guarantees that each gift will be unique. Because the couple themselves has pre-chosen each and every piece, guests are assured their present will be very much wanted . . . and no returns will be necessary!

This works well when the couple has a clear idea of their preferences and knows what their married lifestyle will be. They simply choose personal and household items in a variety of price ranges. These are noted on their Wedding Registry record at a department or gift store. The store keeps tabs of what is bought (sometimes by computer), and checks these items off the list. So you see, the Wedding Registry not only simplifies gift-giving . . . it makes duplication almost impossible. (For a more detailed description of what a wedding registry is and how it works, see our SHOWERWISE STEPS.)

If you want to add a bit of fun to gift-opening, inform guests that since the couple already knows what they've chosen, there's going to be a little guessing fun. Ask them to pack the presents in odd-sized boxes or to wrap them in unusual ways . . . any disquise that may keep the couple from guessing the contents.

Each gift card should also give a clue to what the package holds. For instance the gift card for a dinner place setting could say, "Get set for good eating!" An electric mixer's card might proclaim, "There's been a slight mix-up!" Guests can also play the game . . . and win a small prize if they guess an item before the couple does.

By the way, if the wedding couple's preferences lean in a specific direction, a wedding registry can be set up in ANY type store. We heard of a couple in their fifties who planned a honeymoon bike-hike through the north-eastern states. A bicycle shop handled their wedding registry. No one was more surprised than the store owner . . . and we might add . . . delighted, as well.

GREENHOUSE SHOWER

Think of this shower as providing a splendid backdrop or decor for the couple's living quarters. Plants, flowers and greenery of all kinds, and in all shapes and sizes, are most welcomed by plant lovers.

Containers are important too. If you think the couple would enjoy the unusual—gold fish bowls, mason jars, ice buckets, glass insulators, jewelry boxes, stemmed glassware, mugs and wicker baskets are a few ideas that can give any plant a delightful permanent home.

Carry the idea over to your refreshment table. You can dress up a flower and candle centerpiece with small garden tools, seed packets, floral clay, tape and wire, watering can, fertilizer sticks and other related items.

An idea for an activity is one we heard of from Lucy Oxberry of San Diego, California. Guests are asked to think of flower and plant names that are related to love and marriage. Get them started with these: Everlasting, Bridal Wreath, Love-In-A-Puff, Passion Flower, Silver Bell, Rose, Nosegay and Forget-Me-Not. Give a small prize for each contribution the group judges to be authentic. If any one says, "Tulips" (two lips) . . . they deserve a bonus.

POSTAL SHOWER

When the wedding couple is married in a far off state and most of the home-town crowd won't be able to attend any of the festivities, a postal shower can be a nice surprise. This is promoted either by written invitation or by telephone.

Here's the process. Set a date for the shower. Write or phone the couple, asking them to be at a given place on a certain day and time. Instruct everyone to mail a present so it will arrive well before that date. The outer wrapping should declare, "Do not open until 6:30 p.m. on September 17!" (whatever day and time you've selected). Plan a gathering in your town for the same time. About half an hour after guests have assembled, telephone the couple, long distance, for an exchange of greetings and to extend your best wishes.

If you tell friends and family in the other state what you're planning, they may also want to hold a shower for the couple at the same time, in conjunction with yours. Though this shower spans two states, it's perfect for bringing loved ones together in a most surprising way.

CHERISHED-GIFT SHOWER

Filled with light-hearted touches, this shower passes down the heirlooms from one generation to the next. Family members gather together in celebration to hand over antiques, collectibles, mementos and family treasures to the bride and groom for safekeeping.

As each piece is presented—monogrammed items, cut glass, dinnerware, jewelry—a little of its history is recalled by senior family members. Was the Medal of Honor really presented to grandfather by the President? Was this the brooch great-grandmother wore at her very own wedding? Every family has memories as well as material possessions. To recall these memories at this time gives special meaning to the gifts and fosters appreciation of them.

This shower works especially well for small families, where descendants are few. A maiden-aunt or bachelor-uncle of an only child would love this formal opportunity to pass along such heart-felt gifts.

LEND-A-HAND SHOWER

Here's a shower that's built around year-long help for the couple. Guests give "coupons" for their services—good anytime during the first year of wedded life—instead of the usual presents.

The range is only limited to the special talents and expertise of your guests. Services might include: furniture making or refinishing, budget planning, yard work, appliance repair, auto work, tax help, or simply teaching the couple a decorative or handy skill. Fran Maloney of Fridley, Minnesota tells us her daughter made coupons good for a car wash, house sitting, window cleaning and . . . babysitting "when the time comes!"

Purchase a file box, index cards and blank file guides. Print or type the subject headings on the guides in alphabetical order (appliance repair, auto work, budget planning, etc.). This will be the start of a "help in need" filing system for the couple, so give them a good supply of blank guides to list their own contacts for services your guests don't supply.

~COUPON~
Service: Jay Help
From: John Doe
Address: 111 Pleasant St.
Phone: 800 - 1234

Decorate enough index cards with a "coupon" border so you can send from one to three to each guest, along with the invitation. These don't have to be fancy. A few squiggly lines and the word, "coupon" are fine (as illustrated). This helps the couple immediately identify the shower gift . . . and brings back memories of helpful and giving friends and family.

GIFTS-AROUND-THE-CLOCK SHOWER

To say this shower is "timely" may be stretching a point, but timely it is. Sue Norby of Eau Claire, Wisconsin, tells us the idea is to state in your invitation that each guest bring a gift the couple might use at a certain time of day. Every invitation must specify a different hour (See? Timely!).

Couple your request with four lines of verse and you'll have an invitation that will bring in both practical and fun gifts (printer-ready copy in our INVITATION GUIDE). Here's what we have in mind: If you choose any of the following hours, these suggestions can be passed along to guests who may call you for ideas:

7:30 AM to 8:30 AM—Coffee pot, bud vase, subscription to morning newspaper

8:30 AM to 9:30 AM—Breakfast-in-bed trays, toaster, morning-shower towels

Noon to 1:00 PM—Dishes, napkins, placemats

5:00 PM to 6:00 PM—Blender, electric fry pan, casserole dishes

7:30 PM to 8:30 PM—Magazine subscription, wine glasses, throw pillows

9:30 PM to 10:30 PM—Sleepwear, automatic TV selector, blankets

SHOWERWISE SPRINKLES

"Hold on a minute!" exclaimed ShowerWise. "Is this going to be a handy little book or one of those heavy tomes?"

"Strictly handy and meant to be used," we replied, "but we need a few suggestions for the people who just want a bit...a gem...a germ of an idea more to build on."

ShowerWise cupped their chubby chins in their hands while we kept on talking.

"Just as every party starts with an idea," we continued thoughtfully, "every shower starts with...a..."

"...A Sprinkle!" they chimed, throwing up their arms.

"Just a few more ideas off the top of your curly heads," we coaxed, "maybe three or four."

"How about twenty-four?" they said with a wink.

And here they are...

COLLECTIBLE SHOWER

If you know a couple who suffers from "acquisition" mania, indulge them with a shower of their favorite things. Any addition to their collection—old magazines, coins, dolls, etc. —will bring down their fever.

LAS VEGAS DICE-THROW SHOWER

All those closet gamblers, including bingo addicts, will get into the act on this one. Rent equipment and talk a few friends into providing a little action behind the tables. You'll have the makings of a glamorous Las Vegas night.

CORNUCOPIA SHOWER

Hold a shower of kitchen staples—flour, sugar, vinegar, oil, canned or packaged goods—all giftable and extremely welcome in view of today's grocery prices. Send your invitation in shopping list form and let guests decide which items will best stock the couple's kitchen shelves.

HERB-AND-SPICE SHOWER

Here's a good solution when you want the minimum in gifts and the maximum in guests. Ask everyone, by written or casual invitation, to bring a particular herb or spice. Provide a decorated rack or cabinet for display at the shower. It will make a compact carry-home tote for the guest of honor, with all jars neatly nestled inside.

CANDLELIGHT SHOWER

Candlelight and romance go together like love and marriage. Suggest any and all kinds of candles for the gift list, even candle-making kits. Use plenty of candles and low lights at the shower itself. Evening, of course, is best for this romantic party.

SHEET-MUSIC SHOWER

Use appropriate piano sheet music, dated from the 20's or 30's, such as "The Wedding of the Painted Doll," and build your theme around the lyrics. For this particular one, you might bring out antique or collector dolls. Or buy a brand new bridal doll to use as the focal point of your gift table, along with the original sheet music. Very nostalgic.

BIO-RHYTHM SHOWER

If you have access to a home computer, printer, and a bio-rhythm program, you can build a very interesting shower around them. People always like hearing about themselves, so check out everyone's chart for a special day in their lives. And be sure to plot the couple's bio-rhythms for the wedding day! Also, chart everyone's bio-rhythm and send each guest their chart for the day of the shower. If they're going to have a bad day, tell them they're invited but they can't come. Just kidding, of course!

FABULOUS-FORTIES SHOWER

How's this for a memory jogger: Big band sounds—Harry James, Glen Miller, Benny Goodman; war bonds; Chattanooga Choo Choo; and Frank Sinatra at the Paramount? Is it all coming back? A dress-like-the-forties wedding shower can be lots of fun . . . especially if the "older folk" are in on the planning. Send your invitation in the form of a 78 or 45 RPM record. It's important to keep the saddle shoes moving, so plan a surprise jitterbug contest where all contestants win ribbon awards . . . for style, for enthusiasm, for persistence, for breath control, etc., etc. And oh yes . . . for just plain guts!

NIFTY-FIFTIES SHOWER

Another oldie can be planned along the same lines as the "Fabulous-Forties" shower. Only this time, you can probably get some planning advice from your younger aunts and uncles, instead of your parents. Write your invitation on a pair of sunglasses . . . and here we go: Elvis Presley's rock and roll, cherry cokes, pink and gray color scheme, poodle skirts worn with yards and yards of crinoline slip underneath, gum, gum, gum . . . AND a rousing Dick Clark sock-hop!

CHRISTMAS-BAUBLE SHOWER

Trim their first Christmas tree with gifts of fancy bulbs and other decorations. Handmade and personalized are best, but shiny, satin and new are also very acceptable. Then if each guest adds a treasured ornament from their own stockpile, it should fill out the couple's first Christmas tree rather nicely.

HEALTH-FOOD-HARVEST SHOWER

Ever been invited to a shower by a Vitamin? An invitation featuring a vitamin E capsule (for sexy) gets this one off the ground. You can serve anything from a peanut casserole to a veggie, fruit and cheese salad bar, along with bran muffins. If the honored couple is into health food as a way of life, this shower's tailor-made, especially when combined with a health food recipe exchange.

OPEN-DOOR SHOWER

Why not transform the popular open house party into an "Open-Door" shower? On arrival, present your guests with our "Rose Bud" name tag (see our FAVORS GUIDE), and have the wedding couple open each gift on-the-spot. Lay out an attractive refreshment buffet and help your guests enjoy each other to the tune of soft, background music.

LET'S-GET-CANNED SHOWER

How about showering the wedding couple with gifts that come in cans? Yes, yes, we know—a can of vegetables, a can of fruit, etc., etc. But what about a can of paint to spruce up a room? . . . or a can of anti-freeze or oil for their car? . . . or even a can of tennis balls? What's more, there are novelty stores around the country that will do the honors for you. Buy anything you like and have it canned, while-you-wait!

TAILGATE SHOWER

After the softball, soccer or football game, how about a little tailgating? Spread out your grub around a motor home or several hatch-back cars, get out the lounge chairs and bring your gifts along. Use the newspaper sports page for wrappings and have yourself a ball . . . in the "private room" you've set up.

FILE-AND-FIND-IT SHOWER

When it's time to pay bills, the wedding couple can be tax years ahead of the rest of us if you shower them with a filing cabinet, file folders, tabs, paper clips, stapler and anything else it'll take to get them organized. Be sure to include one of the popular "how-to-get-organized" books. You'll save them so much time, they'll probably want to spend some of it partying with their far-sighted friends.

✒ HERITAGE THEME GALLERY ✒

SCANDINAVIAN SHOWER

"Smorgasbord" is the key word here. Whether of appetizers, a full meal, or simply desserts . . . smorgasbord is a must. For an hors d'oeuvres appetizer table, serve hot and cold meats, smoked and pickled fish, sausages, cheeses, salads and relishes . . . and lefse or flatbread.

MEXICAN SHOWER

Viva La Mexico with large, colorful paper flowers and pinatas for decorations, a serape for your table covering, and a menu of tacos, enchiladas, arroz con pollo and tostada salad for ole' refreshment!

GERMAN SHOWER

Toast the fraulein and herrn with German beer and "gemutlich heit!" Dress your table with flower-laden beer steins, and if possible, find a pretty cuckoo clock for the centerpiece. Polka music played in the background is a must. Serve bratwurst, German potato salad and sauerkraut with plenty of beer. Give one great gift from all—a feather comforter from Germany.

ITALIAN SHOWER

Build your shower around a typical, leisurely Italian meal with at least five courses. Start with an antipasto tray containing rolled up slices of salami, ham, prosciutto, swiss cheese and provolone, all thinly sliced. Add black olives and roasted peppers to complete the tray. Subsequent courses are minestrone soup, lasagna with meatballs and sausages, salad with oil and vinegar dressing, fruit, nuts, and spumoni ice cream or Italian pastries. Serve lots of crusty Italian bread and a good red wine. Rest between courses for hearty conversation and performances by the children.

HAWAIIAN SHOWER

Serve a lush luau at the beach or around the pool. Roll out the straw mats and supply pillow seating for this hearty meal. Serve sweet-and-sour dishes, fresh fruit, rum-and-fruit drinks, pineapple sticks and orange slices. Hire a specialist to teach your guests the hula and another to strum the uke-lele with familiar songs everyone can sing together.

ORIENTAL SHOWER

Exchange your guest's shoes for paper slippers and seat them on floor pillows around a low table. Serve a shrimp and vegetable stir-fry dinner . . . and don't forget the fortune cookies. Decorate with paper lamps and use Oriental background music. For your table centerpiece, try to find a wooden cricket house (for good luck) or a jolly Buddha (for happiness). Provide chopsticks for your more adept guests.

SONG-OF-INDIA SHOWER

Plan lots of bright, hot colors for your gift and buffet tables. Use silk scarves as table accents over a bamboo mat. Display brass, carved ivory or wood accessories. Put on your sari and serve a curry and rice dish. Indian music and burning incense will transport you to this gentle world.

ENGLISH-TEA SHOWER

Wish the happy couple good health and best wishes with an English-tea party. Bring out your collection of assorted china tea cups and serve an assortment of teas and finger sandwiches. A vase or bowl of flowers to set off your table would be ver-r-ry English.

ERIN-GO-BRAGH SHOWER

M-m-m . . . Irish coffee and a rich chocolate dessert gives this shower flavor. Plenty of shamrocks, paper elves (better known as "the little people") and green and white crepe paper streamers set the tone. Favor each guest with an Irish boast-button found in most drug and gift stores. "Thank God I'm Irish" and "Kiss me, I'm Irish" are two of our favorites. Complete the picture with a homemade Blarney Stone and have each guest offer some tongue-in-cheek marriage advice. Faith & begorra . . . what a time we'll have!

SHOWERWISE STEPS

To tell you the truth, we got a little nervous when we thought about this part. After all, we knew you'd be counting on us to give you the very best basic advice, in light of all the shower changes taking place.

Well, of course, we needn't have worried. ShowerWise took us by the hand and walked us through each step until we had a complete plan. And that's what we're going to do for you right now. All the how-to's are here, right down to "protocol" for the couple-to-be. Ready? Here we go . . .

12 STEPS TO A SUCCESSFUL SHOWER

How would you like to reduce pre-party panic feelings to just a few minor jitters? It is possible if you have a good plan and get yourself organized in all major areas. The key is organization.

The best way we know of to take the pressure off is the checklist system. Make a complete checklist for every detail. If necessary, make a list for each day, and especially the day and hours before your shower. When you know you're accomplishing necessary things every day, your enthusiasm will remain high. You won't think . . . not even for a minute . . . "WHY did I get myself into this?".

With a well thought-out plan, you'll have ample time to arrange for extra help and to borrow or rent whatever you need. You may even be able to "take five" before your guests arrive because you've already checked on the ice cubes and coped with last minute emergencies. Then, if anyone offers to help, you'll be so organized, you can assign things they'll enjoy . . . and you can relax and enjoy your own party.

Use these steps, along with our SHOWER PLANNING SHEET, themes and guides to help you plan your party easily and successfully.

1) GUESTS: Consult with the wedding couple, their parents, the bridal party and other friends to ensure a complete guest list.

2) TIME: Select the day and hour of your shower while you're clearing the guest list. Make sure the principal guests can attend.

3) THEME: Browse through our SHOWERWISE THEMES and SHOWERWISE SPRINKLES for a plan you think everyone will enjoy.

4) LOCATION: Pick a location that will accommodate the number of potential guests and that will work in with your theme (private home, VFW hall, church, pool. See our UNUSUAL LOCATIONS GUIDE).

5) INVITATIONS: Invitations may be purchased or hand-made (see our INVITATIONS GUIDE for ideas). Mail them to arrive at least two weeks before your shower date. Include this information, as well as further directions or instructions:
• FOR (name of persons being honored)
• DATE (before or after the wedding)
• TIME (when most convenient for everyone)
• PLACE (location of shower—home, hall, pool, etc.)
• KIND (kitchen, personal, general, theme, etc.)

- WEDDING REGISTRY AT (location of store)
- GIVEN BY (hostess or host)
- R.S.V.P. (name and phone number of person to call for acceptance or "Regrets Only")

6) FOOD: Decide who will prepare the food: you; a caterer; restaurant; your guests; etc. If you engage someone else to do it, have a clear understanding of exactly what will be provided and the cost. If you will be doing it, plan every detail. Make a shopping list from your recipes and do as much as you can ahead of time. Be sure your kitchen facilities can handle everything you've planned to prepare at the time of your shower (enough oven and surface burner space, ample room in the refrigerator). Plan your silverware, plates, salad bowls, dessert dishes, glasses, cups and saucers, serving dishes, ash trays, candle holders, etc. (See our FOOD-TABLE SET-UP GUIDE for how-to set up a buffet, a sit-down dinner and a dessert only table.)

7) DECORATIONS: Choose decorations that will give your shower area a festive look. Include favors, name tags and place cards in your thinking—they can help your guests get acquainted. Browse through floral centers and department, novelty, hardware and gift stores for ideas. Tell salespeople what you're planning and ask for their help (see our DECORATIONS GUIDE, too). It's customary in some places to provide small corsages for the bride-to-be, her mother, and future mother-in-law.

8) GAMES: Plan your games and collect the equipment you'll need (pencils, dice, etc.). Purchase suitable prizes. There are shower game books in gift stores that contain not only ideas, but actual game sheets for each guest. Look for our own GAMES FOR WEDDING SHOWER FUN book for the latest in shower games.

9) ACTIVITIES: Buy or make the props you'll need (e.g., if you're planning a recipe exchange, have plenty of 3"x 5" index cards and pens available. Look over our ACTIVITIES GUIDE for ideas, too.

10) ADDED ATTRACTIONS: Plan or arrange any added attractions. If you're bringing in live entertainment, you'll need to clear your date with them. It's also wise to sign a simple, but specific, contract. Select stereo music, special lighting and other items beforehand. And look through our ADDED ATTRACTIONS GUIDE for special touches.

11) HELPERS: Contact guests you know well to help you run your shower smoothly.

12) RELAX AND ENJOY!

SHOWER PLANNING SHEET

1) GUEST LIST (Use separate sheet for additional names)

1 _____

2 _____

3 _____

4 _____

5 _____

6 _____

7 _____

8 _____

9 _____

10 _____

11 _____

12 _____

2) DATE _____

TIME: From _____ To _____

3) THEME _____

   Special preparations needed _____

   _____

4) LOCATION _____

   Address _____

   Phone # _____ Contract signed _____

5) INVITATIONS   Addressed _____ Mailed _____

   R.S.V.P. to _____ Phone _____

   Wedding Registry at _____

   Gift type preference _____

6) FOOD (Also make a grocery list from your recipes)

   Buffet _____ Sit down _____

   MENU: Brunch   Dinner   Dessert Only

7) DECORATIONS (Also make a separate list of items you
   must purchase)

ROOM _____

SERVING TABLE _____

GIFT-OPENING AREA _____

SPECIAL CHAIR _____

GUEST-OF-HONOR _____

GUESTS _____

ORDER CORSAGE FOR: _____

   Ordered   ____   _____

   Picked up ____   _____

HELPERS: _____

FAVORS (keepsake) _____
(Favor may also serve as name tag or place card)

8) GAMES (if any):

1 _____

Prize _____

Equipment needed _____

_____

2 _____

Prize _____

Equipment needed _____

_____

_____

3 _____

Prize _____

Equipment needed _____

_____

GAME HELPERS _____

_____

(Helpers can give directions, distribute and collect equipment, create enthusiasm and keep things moving.)

9) ACTIVITIES (if any): _____

1 _____

Preparations _____

_____

2 _____

Preparations _____

_____

ACTIVITIES HELPERS _____

_____

10) ADDED ATTRACTIONS (if any):

1 _____

Preparations _____

_____

2 _____

Preparations _____

_____

Phone # _____

Contract signed _____

(Introduce performers before, and thank them after performance)

SHARED SHOWER PROTOCOL . . .

. . . FOR THE SHOWER HOSTESS (or HOST)

As the party giver, you'll naturally want to make your
guests as comfortable as possible. Most often, all you need
to do is be sure there's a way each person can meet others.
You can do this either through personal introduction, name
tags, or get-acquainted games and activities. If you also
mention each guest's relationship to the bride-or-groom-to-
be, you'll give your guests a "conversation starter" they'll
appreciate.

Take the guests-of-honor under your wing and let them
know exactly what you've planned. Many young couples are
in need of help, especially if it's their first shower.

Arrange a gift-opening area and let them know when they
should begin opening presents. Ask two helpers (usually
members of the bridal party) to sit on either side of the
guest-of-honor: one to keep gift and gift card together after
opening, and to pass it around for guests to take a closer
look; the other to gather the wrappings and to make a keepsake ribbon bouquet (see our DECORATIONS GUIDE).
Designate one other person to inconspicuously write down
each gift and giver's name on a sheet of paper. This will

make "thank-you note time" much easier, especially when combined with the "Party-Giver Gift" in our GIFT GUIDE.

In a nutshell, then, if you concentrate on making others as comfortable as possible, nothing serious can go wrong.

...FOR THE INTENDED COUPLE

Your host(ess), relatives and friends have planned a special occasion for YOU...a wedding shower. They've come together to rejoice in your intended wedding because they love you and want you to begin your marriage with warm and happy memories, as well as material gifts. Yes, you're the honored guests, but you also have certain responsibilities. Nothing heavy...just a few hints.

If you're at all squeamish about the occasion, confide in your host(ess) and ask for help. He or she wants to make everything as lovely as possible for you and will willingly assist. Or perhaps your parents, parents-in-law-to-be, or a favorite relative can give you some advice. The point is, if you're not sure how to conduct yourself, many helpful people are available who would be flattered that you asked.

Probably the most important thing you can do is to let each guest know, in some way, how much you appreciate the time, energy and expense they've exerted on your behalf. All it takes is spending a few moments with each person... just chatting. See? Very easy for you, but it will mean a great deal to them.

Gift-opening time is when you'll have the stage all to yourself, but, again, help is near. If no spot has been pre-arranged, find a place to sit down where everyone will be able to see you. As you open each gift and hold it up for everyone to see, say a few words. Your remarks should be personal and directed toward each giver. Naturally, you'll extend your thanks. It's also nice to mention how the gift will be used. Here are some remarks we've heard that were especially nice:

"This fits our bedroom color scheme beautifully!"

"We like to cook together and this will make it even more fun!"

"We really need this!"

"This is just the right size to fit on our counter!"

Just take your time, choose your words, and do your best to acknowledge each gift and giver.

Now, suppose you've already got ten thing-a-lings and here's another one staring you in the face? We suggest you say your thanks, along with other appropriate remarks and then talk with the giver later, and in private, to arrange an exchange. Perhaps your host(ess) will help you here.

Finally, as soon as possible after the shower, write "Thank-You" notes using the same hints we gave you for gift-opening: mention the gift, how it will be used, and say your sincere thanks. AND—don't forget to write a special note to your host(ess). Your thanks can pin-point the lovely time you had, the effort and expense you know the shower took, the useful gifts you received, and the good start you'll have now, because of this special shower.

Do you feel ready? Good, because we really want you to shine!

THE WEDDING REGISTRY SERVICE

Long known as The Bridal Registry, the name seems to be gradually changing because of the current involvement of men in household matters. More and more couples are making decisions together in this important area.

At the registry, trained personnel will assist the wedding couple make their "wish list" become a reality, according to their combined tastes. They help them choose items that friends and relatives are most likely to purchase. They point out items the couple may not have thought of and show them brands with which they may not be familiar. In many stores, this is done on computer and copies of the printout are available. After the list is completed, the couple or their families pass the word on to friends and relatives.

The Wedding Registry not only saves time but has other advantages. People can go directly to the named store to select a gift. They can even order by phone and have it wrapped and delivered. There is no duplication. They know the gift is something the couple wants. And as a bonus, in most cases the list is saved and can then be consulted for birthday, anniversary and other holiday gifts.

Encourage the wedding couple to choose a store that sells merchandise closely resembling their tastes. Most registries are in department and gift stores, but the manager of any type store will more than likely be happy to set one up.

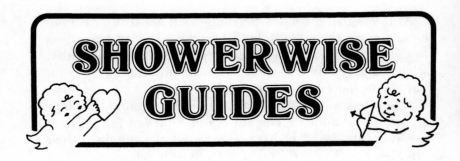

SHOWERWISE GUIDES

When we started this section, we suddenly realized our book was almost completed . . . and it sure had a quieting effect on us. But, there came ShowerWise. They were laughing and frolicking in mid-air, just bursting to tell us the good news!

"This last part's going to be a veritable gold mine!" they shouted, shooting off their arrows like fireworks. "Dramatic decorations, attention-getting invitations, uncommon favors, gift ideas galore, and more, more, more!"

Naturally, we grabbed our pencils and took it all down. Well, we think you'll agree, they really outdid themselves!

ACTIVITIES GUIDE

IDEAS FROM SHOWER THEMES
- Have a craft, napkin folding, cake decorating, etc., demonstration and let your guests take part . . . as in "Show-Me" shower.

FOLDING TABLE NAPKINS
(For demonstration or decoration)

CACTUS FOLD
DIRECTIONS
Fold napkin into four parts.
Fold square into triangle.
Pleat from A to B.
Pull down the four leaves.

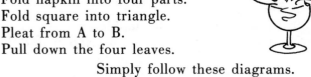

Simply follow these diagrams.

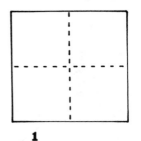

PALM LEAF FOLD
DIRECTIONS
Fold square napkins into four parts.
Fold diagonally across but make the fold a little off-center
so as to form the base of the napkin fold.
Pleat evenly and place the base of the napkin into the nap-
kin ring.
Set the napkin and ring upright on the plate.

Simply follow these diagrams.

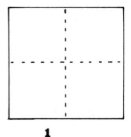 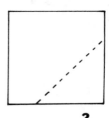 

CASCADE FOLD
DIRECTIONS

Fold napkin in four parts.

Bring back free corner H to opposite corner D; finger press.

Fold back next free corner G to C.

Fold corner F to point B and corner E to point A, finger pressing each fold.

Fold corner E back to base line of napkin.

Fold edges X and Y back until the edges overlap behind the napkin.

Tuck a red carnation in the top fold of napkin.

Simply follow these diagrams.

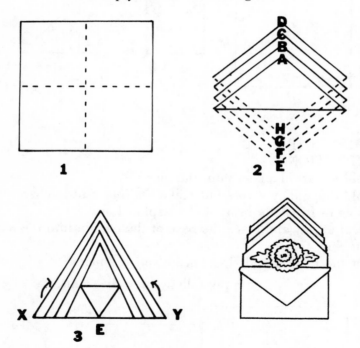

ROSE FOLD
DIRECTIONS

Fold points A of square napkin to center B.

Repeat with new corners C that were just made. (Design will get smaller each time although diagrams are full size for convenience.)

Turn napkin over and bring corners E to center F.

Holding down center with a straight edge cup or glass, reach under at points G and lift each doubled corner up and over to center.

Finally, pull out at points I for remaining petals.

Simply follow these diagrams.

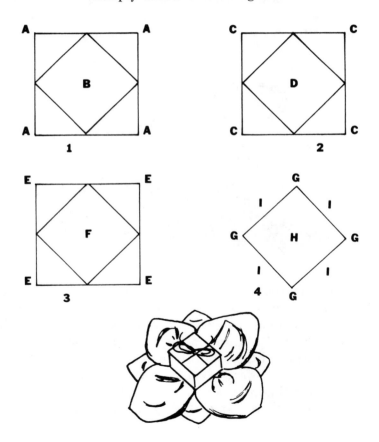

- Make a corsage from ribbon and netting. Instead of using flowers, fasten small kitchen items to it. Ask the intended bride or bridegroom to explain how each item is used . . . as in "Shower-On-A-Shoestring."
- Guests form a wide circle around the intended couple. Each person says a few words of congratulations to them. Then everyone swoops in for handshaking, kisses and hugs . . . as in "Sunday-Go-To-Meeting" shower.
- Take instant photos during the shower and slip them into an album on-the-spot. This makes a nice remembrance gift for the wedding couple . . . as in "Sunday-Go-To-Meeting" shower.
- Fill a suitcase with pennies (nickels, dimes, dollars?) and have guests estimate the total amount enclosed. Winning guess gets a prize and the wedding couple gets a surprise gift . . . as in "Another Idea" following "Pounding-Party" shower.

- Gather snapshots, home movies, high school and college year books, scrapbooks, pennants, awards, trophies, etc., of the wedding couple's growing-up years . . . as in "Home-From-The-Honeymoon," "Meet-The-Relatives" and "Surprise-Friendship" showers.
- Record your shower on audio or video cassette and present this lasting keepsake to the wedding couple . . . as in "Hollywood Stars" and "College Soap-Opera" showers.

- Housewives and househusbands—hold your shower during your favorite soap-opera with other addicts . . . as in "College Soap-Opera" shower.
- To prepare the couple for "rice-throwing-time" at their wedding, wind up your fun shower by blowing soap bubbles at them . . . as in "College Soap-Opera" shower.
- Ask guests to fill 3"x 5" index cards with their favorite recipes. Punch two holes along the tops of all of them and tie with a pretty ribbon . . . as in "Share-A-Menu" shower.
- Distribute 3"x 5" cards to your guests and ask them to jot down one or two handy household hints for the couple . . . as in "Handy-Andy/Hardware-Hannah" shower.
- If your shower's held at a pool, lake or beach, get the adrenaline flowing with some balloon antics . . . as in "Apartment/Condo Pool" shower.
- Show home movies of the bride-and-groom-to-be in their growing-up years . . . as in "Meet-The-Relatives" shower.
- Supply your guests with white plastic garbage bags and have them make their own congratulatory aprons . . . as in "Wok-On-The-Wild-Side" shower, or their vests . . . as in "No-Sweat" shower (see our DECORATIONS GUIDE).

- How many flowers and plant names can your guests think of that relate to love and marriage? Everytime someone comes up with a good one during the shower, give a small prize . . . as in "Greenhouse" shower.

- Make a "Laugh-Ah-Meter" to gauge your guests' reaction to any activity that calls for impromptu remarks ... as in "Pounding-Party" shower.

- Supply each guest with a square of pellon (found in fabric stores) and a marking pen. Ask them to print the one word they think is most important in a marriage. Then glue all squares together and you've made a keepsake wall hanging for the couple ... as in "Tie-A-Quilt" shower.
- Throw a foreign-food shower. There's a whole section, centered around delightful eating ... as in our "Heritage Theme Gallery" in SHOWERWISE, SPRINKLES.
- Fill a 24" square container with wet plaster of Paris. Have guests leave a thumb print and sign their names in it. When dry, it's a remembrance plaque for the couple ... as in "Hollywood Stars" shower.
- Take a large poster board and write "Marriage Advice From Your Family and Friends" across the top. During your shower, ask guests to jot down a few words ... as in "Home-From-The-Honeymoon" shower.

INVITATIONS GUIDE

If you use one of our printer-ready invitations, simply cut inside the broken line and have your local print shop reproduce as many copies as you need. You may purchase standard-sized envelopes there, or wherever stationery is sold. A good quality copy machine may also be used to reproduce our invitations.

Printer ready invitations can be found immediately following invitations guide.

IDEAS FROM SHOWER THEMES

- For any shower held poolside, at the beach, lake or on a boat, write your invitation on an inflatable childrens' life preserver . . . as in "Apartment/Condo Pool" shower.
- Balloon-A-Grams, flower bouquets and singing telegrams are all invitations with flair . . . as in "The Elegant" and "Formal Pool" showers.
- Pin invitations to T-shirts with appropriate designs (wedding bells, hearts) and ask guests to wear them to your shower, where they'll become part of your decorations . . . as in "No-Sweat" shower.
- For an informal shower, write your invitation on a pullover vest made from white plastic garbage bags. Tell guests to wear them to your shower where they'll become part of your decorations . . . as in "No-Sweat" shower (see our DECORATIONS GUIDE).
- Want to get your prospective guests' attention? Write your invitation on a fan! . . . as in "Wok-On-The-Wild-Side" shower.
- An attention-getting invitation makes you the clever one! Do yours up on plastic wine glasses . . . as in "Wine-And-Cheese-Tasting" shower.

OTHER IDEAS

- Print on tennis balls, paper dishes or any unusual surface for eye-catching invitations.
- Frost your invitation on large cookies or lollipops. Confectioner's icing will do the job.
- Tuck an invitation into a balloon with directions to pop it on arrival.
- Cut and paste words, phrases and pictures from magazines and newspapers to get your message across.
- Buy cards with an appropriate photo or illustration on the cover and blank on the inside. Just script in our verse or your own.

IRIS FOLD INVITATION
(See "SHOW-ME" SHOWER)
DIRECTIONS
Fold napkin in half, A to B, to form a triangle.

Take C and fold to AB. Do the same with D to make a diamond shape.

Every diamond has four points. In this case only one of the points has completely folded edges. Use this point as F and fold not quite to E to form a kind of triangle again.

Fold F down to I.

Turn napkin over; tuck one point into the other behind the triangle.

Turn the napkin again and drape the two top points to each side to form petals. Leave the remaining point upright.

Pen invitation on napkin as shown.

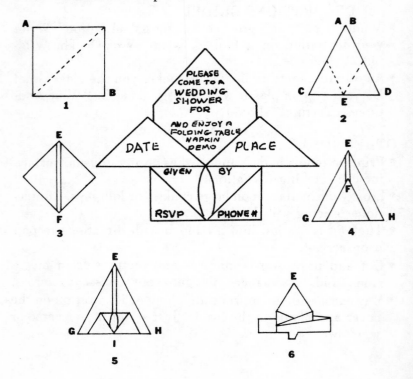

PRINTER-READY INVITATIONS

"MEET-THE-RELATIVES" SHOWER

Please come to a family shower....
Won't you join us, please
We're about to unite
Two family trees!

FOR: _____

DATE: _____

TIME: _____

PLACE: _____

GIVEN BY: _____

R.S.V.P. _____

Simply cut inside the broken line.

"BE-MY-VALENTINE" SHOWER

You're invited . . .
Cupid brought them together
And soon they'll be one,
Come to this Valentine shower
And join in the fun!

FOR: _____

DATE: _____

TIME: _____

PLACE: _____

KIND: _____

WEDDING REGISTRY AT: _____

GIVEN BY: _____

R.S.V.P. _____

Simply cut inside the broken line.

"HANDY-ANDY/HARDWARE-HANNAH" SHOWER

You're Invited To A Wedding Shower

Bring a gadget,
Bring a tool.
Help the new couple,
Keep their cool!

FOR: _____

DATE: _____ TIME: _____

PLACE: _____

WEDDING REGISTRY AT: _____

GIVEN BY: _____

R.S.V.P. _____

Wrap gift in original hardware bag!

Simply cut inside the broken line.

"POUNDING-PARTY" SHOWER

You're invited to a Wedding Shower!

Come "Pound" the couple to give them a start....

a pound of coffee with a coffeemaker
a pound of nuts with a nut dish
a pound of nails with a hammer set
a pound of paper with a pen set

Are all gifts from the heart!

FOR: _____

DATE: _____

TIME: _____

PLACE: _____

WEDDING REGISTRY AT: _____

GIVEN BY: _____ R.S.V.P. _____

Simply cut inside the broken line.

MEMO

OFFICE CO-WORKER SHOWER

TO: All Department Personnel

FROM: The Wedding Shower Committee

RE: Very Important Event!

This memo takes precedent over all other

letters, reports, meetings, etc., etc.!

FOR:

TIME:

PLACE:

Simply cut inside the broken line.

"GIFTS-AROUND-THE-CLOCK" SHOWER

You're invited . . .
The couple's all aglow
With rings and bells and flowers.
Our gifts will show them what to do
With their happy marriage hours.

Please bring a shower gift the couple can use
between _____ and _____.

FOR: _____

DATE: _____

TIME: _____

PLACE: _____

WEDDING REGISTRY AT: _____

GIVEN BY: _____

R.S.V.P. _____

Simply cut inside the broken line.

DECORATIONS GUIDE

DECORATE YOUR ROOM OR SPACE

IDEAS FROM SHOWER THEMES

- Spray almost any household throw-away with gold or silver paint to create a decorative item: jars; cut-off plastic bottles; egg cartons, etc . . . .as in "Handy-Andy/Hardware-Hannah" shower.
- While your shower's still in the planning stage, use your imagination to come up with items that can be used in unusual ways such as in "Wok-On-The-Wild-Side" shower.
- Personalize colored balloons and other decorations by using a permanent marking pen to write the intended couple's names, the wedding date, or the words "Wedding Shower"—or all three . . . as in "Apartment/Condo Pool" shower.
- Check with book stores, travel agencies, gift stores, etc., for posters they receive for display, but don't use. Anything that relates to your theme, or to wedding showers will help you . . . as in "Romantic-Novel" shower.
- Having a shower poolside? Decorate your swimming pool with a large styrofoam heart . . . as in "Formal Pool" shower.
- Fun posters and homemade signs that relate to love and marriage can fill in the bare spots and create a bit of fun . . . as in "Roast-The-Manager" and "Home-From-The-Honeymoon" showers.
- Obtain a copy of the bride and groom's family trees. Have an artist or calligrapher reproduce and frame them. Hang in a prominent place and present it to the couple as a special gift . . . as in "Meet-The-Relatives" shower.

- Enlarge a photo of the bride and groom, paste it on a poster board and print a fun caption on it, such as "Who's Boss?" . . . as in "Roast-The-Manager" shower.

- Have blown-ups made of the couple's baby pictures (on a fur rug?) and display them in a prominent place . . . as in "Meet-The-Relatives" shower.

OTHER IDEAS
- Wedding bells (paper, foil, satin, plastic)
- Small silver "jingle" bells
- Chubby cupids with bows and arrows
- Red, silver or gold hearts
- Colorful flowers (fresh, silk, paper, plastic)
- Ornate paper slippers filled with colored rice
- Bright-colored watering can with silver or gold ribbons streaming from the spout
- Opened parasols or umbrellas (paper, plastic, fabric). Decorate with bows, streamers, flowers.
- Lavish flower garlands or baskets (fresh, silk, paper or plastic flowers)
- Plump balloons (all sizes and shapes)
- Silver or gold-toned wedding rings of all sizes
- Large tied knots (paper, ribbon, foil)
- Multi-colored string confetti and crepe paper streamers
- Sparkly foil, tinsel, sequin material, bead strings
- Champagne fountain

DECORATE YOUR TABLE

Plan your tablesettings by allowing the shower theme, wedding colors, time of season, background colors and use of formal or informal tableware to guide you.

For buffet or sit-down dinners, an ecru or white organza cutwork tablecloth over a light blue liner can be smashing. Carry out the color scheme with blue folded napkins, and use a spray of blue carnations for the centerpiece.

For informal parties with stoneware dishes, use a heavy, solid-colored linen-type cloth (Mardi Gras cloth) with earth tones. Pull in other colors with fabric napkins and a handsome centerpiece.

For theme showers, use the colors and subject matter of the theme. For instance, at a Texas-type cowboy barbecue shower, use red and white checked tablecloth and napkins, straw baskets for bread sticks and serving dishes, and a ceramic cowboy boot for a hefty centerpiece. Make red papier-mache napkin rings (or paint wooden ones) with the couple's names on them (ie., Liz and Ken).

For casual parties, take your choice of the beautifully patterned paper products on the market today. Some of the larger greeting card companies have done the work for you. They've put out whole lines of attractive paper tableware. At most gift stores, you'll find wedding bells, umbrellas, watering cans and other shower-motif centerpieces to start you out. Then the tablecloth, napkins and plates are design and color-coordinated for a "total" look.

IDEAS FROM SHOWER THEMES:

- Watch your table decorate itself! Set a wine rack on it and ask each guest to bring a gift-wrapped bottle of wine or liquor to stock the couple's bar ... as in "Wine-And-Cheese-Tasting" shower.

• "Mirrored Reflection" is the name of an elegant center-piece that can be used when you want a little sparkle ... as in "Dollar-Disco-Dance" shower.

"DOLLAR DISCO DANCE" MIRRORED REFLECTION DIRECTIONS

1) Use a mirror tile square of reflective (silver) placemat as a base.

2) Arrange votive lights (candles) and glass or crystal candle holders of varying heights on it. Then tuck in a small spray of flowers.

3) Print the "DOLLAR DISCO DANCE" card and place it in center, as shown.

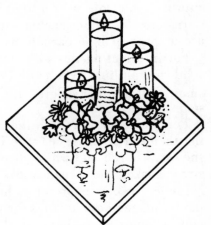

DOLLAR DISCO DANCE SHOWER

for
JANE DOE
and
JOHN SMITH

You have 5 chances to win a prize!
- $1 per   dance -
PLUS
Bankroll DANCE - $5

If you're dancing with the bride and groom when the music suddenly stops—You WIN!

(Listen for M.C.'s instructions)

- Fun-wrapped, smaller gifts can be attractive centerpieces if you have more than one table. As the couple opens each one, the time spent provides an opportunity to chat with guests who are sitting nearby . . . as in "Co-Hostess" shower.
- Ice sculptures (umbrella, watering can, wedding bells) make a dramatic centerpiece for a bountiful buffet . . . as in "The Elegant" and "Second-Time-Around" showers.
- Unusual items that tie in with your theme can be used to create a fascinating centerpiece . . . as in "Handy-Andy/Hardware-Hannah" and "Greenhouse" showers.
- Decorate a cake in the usual way but add your guests' names to it . . . as in "Home-From-The-Honeymoon" shower.

OTHER IDEAS:
- Paste a round of cardboard on the back of an embroidery hoop. Fill with colored rice and set your casserole or other hot dish on it as you would use a hot pad or trivet.
- Personalize napkins, plates, glasses and cups with pens that will write on paper, plastic or metal.
- Fill a wide-mouthed glass with colored rice and push a fat candle down the center.

DECORATE YOUR GIFT-OPENING AREA

IDEAS FROM SHOWER THEMES:
- Spray wire fencing with gold, silver or any color paint to make a nice enclosure for gifts. Do the same with a medium-size barrel and the couple has a nifty take-home container that can later be used as a clothes hamper, or turned upside down to make a cozy table-for-two . . . as in "Handy-Andy/Hardware-Hannah" shower.

- Twist two colors of crepe paper streamers together to rope off an area for gifts . . . as in "Apartment/Condo Pool" shower.
- Combine the color and texture of fresh or silk flower garlands and white satin ribbon for a very classy gift-spot . . . as in "The Elegant" shower.
- Use a folding screen to make a V-type enclosure for gifts . . . as in "Romantic Novel" shower.

"ROMANTIC NOVEL" BACKDROP DIRECTIONS:

1) Paint replica of novel front and back covers on poster boards (fig. 1).

fig. 1

2) Attach posters to two sides of folding screen (1 and 2) and use third side (3) to steady screen (fig. 2). Pile gifts in the V-space (arrow).

fig. 2 ↑

OTHER IDEAS:
- Decorate a large wicker basket with bows. This holds shower gifts at your party and serves as a take-home container for the couple.
- Make and paint a large "wishing-well" replica to hold shower gifts.

THE CHAIR(S)-OF-HONOR

- Decorate a special chair for the guest-of-honor to sit in while opening presents... as in "No-Sweat" shower.

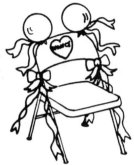

- Decorate two "director's chairs" and seat the intended couple at a 45 degree angle to each other. Pile gifts between them and have them take turns "directing" the action... as in "Hollywood Stars" shower.

THE HONORED COUPLE

- Make a mock top hat and bridal veil for the couple to get them ready for the real thing... as in "College Soap-Opera" shower.

MOCK TOP HAT AND VEIL DIRECTIONS—

VEIL

1) Using a one yard square of netting, sew a basting stitch and gather along dotted line. Fold corner A under gathers (fig. 1).

2) Fasten gathered netting over headband with slipstitch (fig. 2).

3) Secure a string of artificial flowers to headband and netting (fig. 3).

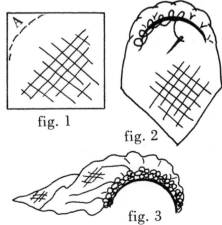

fig. 1

fig. 2

fig. 3

TOP HAT

1) Cut black posterboard to fit around head as shown—A. Cut B and C in proportion (fig. 1).

2) Form a cylinder by rolling A until ends meet. Tape tabs to inside (fig. 2).

3) Insert cylinder into B, taping tabs to inside of cylinder (fig. 3).

4) Tape tabs of C into top of hat as shown (fig. 4).

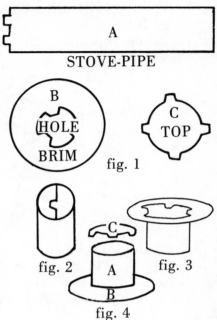

- For an all-in-fun shower, adorn the couple with crazy hats, bow-ties, and more...as in "Roast-The-Manager" shower.
- Make a "Ribbon Bouquet" keepsake for the intended bride out of all the ribbon ties from packages, after gifts have been opened...as in SHOWERWISE STEPS.

RIBBON BOUQUET

DIRECTIONS

1) Cut X through center of paper plate. Draw ribbons of bows thru X.

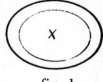

fig. 1

2) Stick self-adhesive bows around outer edge of plate. When entire plate is covered with bows, it resembles a bride's bouquet.

fig. 2

DECORATE YOUR GUESTS

IDEAS FROM SHOWER THEMES:
- Across-the-chest banners can easily be made for or by your guests. Distribute marking pens and strips of paper. Ask them to write a bit of "married-life advice" especially for the couple . . . as in "Calorie-Counter" shower.
- Make congratulatory aprons or vests for guests . . . or have them make their own . . . as in "Wok-On-The-Wild-Side" and "No-Sweat" showers.

"WOK-ON-THE-WILD- SIDE" APRON AND "NO-SWEAT" VEST

APRON DIRECTIONS:
Lay out a large, white, plastic, kitchen garbage bag. In sealed end, cut along curved lines to make head and arm holes, as indicated (fig. 1). Do not cut open end.

VEST DIRECTIONS:
Follow apron directions, except cut from open end, where indicated (fig. 2).

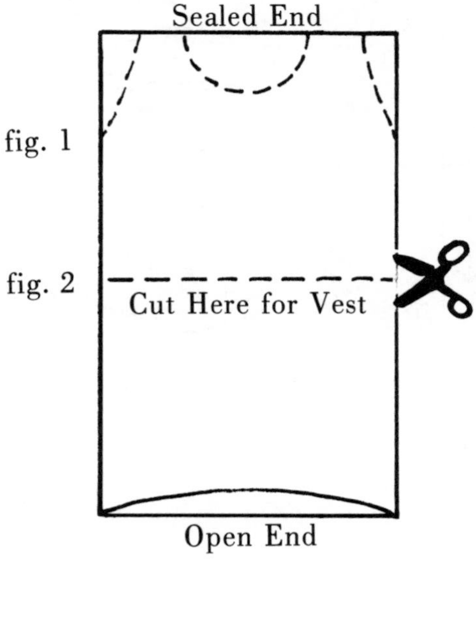

fig. 1

fig. 2

Sealed End

Cut Here for Vest

Open End

FOOD-TABLE SET-UP GUIDE

BUFFET BLUEPRINT

Serve two entrees, fish and beef, one vegetable, one potato or rice dish, condiments, buttered rolls, beverage and
dessert. Arrange a paper umbrella with ribbon and flowers
for a centerpiece.

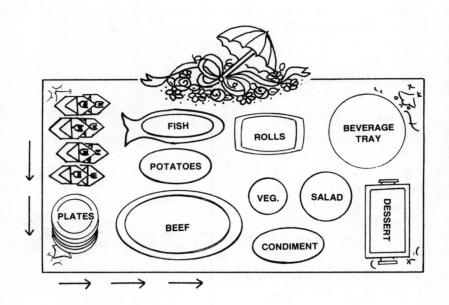

SIT-DOWN DINNER BLUE PRINT

Serve an appetizer, one entree, one vegetable, one pasta, potato or rice, one tossed salad, dinner rolls, beverage and dessert. Decorate each table with wedding bells, one white candle and ribbons.

DESSERT-ONLY BLUEPRINT

Serve a decorated wedding shower cake, bars, bundt cake, coffee, tea, nuts and mints. Choose flowers closely matching the colors of the wedding party for your centerpiece.

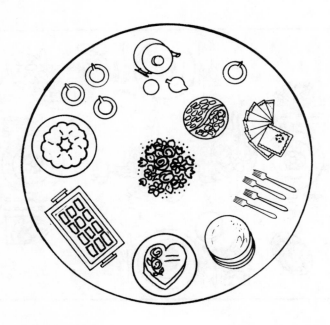

FAVORS, NAME TAG AND PLACE CARD GUIDE

The favor, name tag, and place card can be made in any size and shape. The place card is usually folded to give it a stand. Unfolded, it can set in the plate, napkin fold, or be propped against a favor or glass.

IDEAS FROM SHOWER THEMES:

- Almost any favor, name tag or place card can be numbered in back or underneath as the basis for a door prize drawing ... as in "Another Idea" following "Be-My-Valentine" shower.
- Fill a small square of white netting with colored rice and tie it all up with a pretty ribbon. Pin it to a card and it becomes a name tag. Fold the card and it becomes a place card ... as in "Another Idea" following "Dollar-Disco-Dance" shower.

- Snap instant photos of each guest with the guest-of-honor, or take several group shots for lasting keepsakes ... as in "Surprise-Friendship" shower.
- Refrigerator magnets found in drug and gift stores come with a variety of clever one-liners. Or make your own ... as in "Calorie-Counter" shower.
- Dazzle your guests with a fresh flower, presented in a spectacular napkin fold ... as in "Be-My-Valentine" shower.
- Place a small music box or miniature flower basket at each place setting for a unique favor and/or place card ... as in "The Elegant" shower.

- Fill a heart or bell-shaped cookie cutter with candy or nuts. Tie the whole package together with netting and a plump bow for a favor/place card ... as in "Share-A-Menu" shower.

- Have your guests print their name in the upper left hand corner of the apron/vest favor mentioned in "Decorate Your Guests" and you've created a name tag too ... as in "Wok-On-The-Wild-Side" shower.
- Fill a small rectangular pocket with nylon batting and edge it with lace. Press a shiny address label to it and you've got "Pillow Puff", a very pretty name tag/favor ... as in "Meet-The-Relatives" shower.

"PILLOW PUFF" NAME TAG/FAVOR

DIRECTIONS:

1) Cut two 4"x 3" satin rectangles. With right sides together, sew along dotted line (fig. 1).

2) Turn right side out and fill with nylon batting. Turn unfinished edge inside and sew all around, attaching pre-shirred lace as you go. Sew small bow made from thin satin ribbon to center top (fig. 2).

3) Press a white address label (the permanent, self-adhesive kind) to front (fig. 3).

fig. 1

fig. 2

*Lorraine Olson
Aunt of the Groom*

fig. 3

- Easily make a name tag or place card that features a fresh or silk flower. Ours is called "Rose Bud" . . . as in "Open-Door" shower.

"OPEN-DOOR" ROSE BUD NAME TAG

DIRECTIONS:

Cut card to 1½"x 3½" size. Make two holes with paper punch at arrows. Push flower through holes, stem first, as shown.

Mary Smith
Mother of the Bride

OTHER IDEAS:

- Add drawings, borders, stickers, glitter, shells, sequins, etc., to a white card, construction paper or adhesive-backed label for tailor-made name tags or place cards.
- Cut egg cups out of a plastic or paper egg carton. Spray them silver or gold. Link two together with ribbon, along with a card for a simple place card.

BELLS

DIRECTIONS

1) Punch holes in tops of egg carton cups "bells" and in corner of card.

2) Knot one end of two ribbons and pull up through bells. Lace through card and tie bow.

- Paste or draw wedding shower accessories (umbrella, love birds, watering can, wedding bells, flowers) to name tag or place card.
- Cut a wedding bell from white paper and glue lace around the outline for a simple name tag.

- Tie ribbon around small boxes of white almond candy. Some confectioners have wedding accessory candy and boxes already made up.
- Stretch material over a small embroidery hoop and trim with lace. Applique a heart with the wedding date in the center.
- Take a plastic or wooden curtain ring and paste a round of poster board behind it. Draw a heart and write the wedding date in the center. Tie a bow through the eye for a pin-on name tag.
- Place the goblet or wine glass upside-down at each place setting. Center a small, white or silver doilie on top of it. Display a fresh or silk carnation (with flower pin through stem) on the doilie for a dinner-time favor. Each guest pins one on.

ADDED ATTRACTIONS GUIDE

IDEAS FROM SHOWER THEMES:
- Live background music can do more for your shower atmosphere than an umbrella! The piano, harp, violin, guitar and accordian all lend themselves nicely . . . as in "Be-My-Valentine" and "Second-Time-Around" showers.
- Have the guest-of-honor picked up and delivered to your shower by limousine . . . as in "The Elegant" shower.

OTHER IDEAS:

Background stereo music, magician, clown, juggler, video tape of shower, audio recording of shower, handwriting analyst, on-the-spot computer bio-rhythm printout, craft and cooking demonstrations, synchronized swim program, horse and carriage ride, hay wagon ride, hot-air balloon ride.

GIFT GUIDE

PARTY-GIVER GIFT

- Here's a great party-giver gift! Purchase thank-you notes. Address an envelope to each guest and apply postage. Present these to the honored guest and tell him/her, that each gift card and thank-you note will be tucked into the appropriate gift. When it's time to write "thank-you's," half the work will be done. This gesture is especially appreciated because of the many details the couple is faced with before the wedding . . . as in SHOWERWISE STEPS.

IDEAS FROM SHOWER THEMES:
- When you're holding a "kitchen" shower, ask guests to include a favorite recipe with their gift . . . as in "Cookie-Sampler" shower.
- To direct gift-giving, the obvious solution is the Wedding Registry . . . as in "Wedding Registry" shower and SHOWERWISE STEPS.
- Want to hand down heirlooms at your shower? Make it meaningful . . . as in "Cherished-Gift" shower.
- Is the wedding couple getting married in another state? You can be there . . . as in "Postal" shower.
- Every shower doesn't have to call for material gifts. Some people would rather give of themselves by offering their services . . . as in "Lend-A-Hand" shower.

OTHER IDEAS:

- Home Furnishings: towels, bathroom scale, pillows, bedspread, curtains, extension cords—regular and heavy duty, plants, hamper, flashlight, one box of miscellaneous household needs (scissor, twine, scotch tape, masking tape, paper clips, index cards, hammer, screwdriver, screws, nails, tacks picture hangers), cleaning supplies and rags, large box of rolls of toilet tissue, paper towels or any paper product.

- Personal Gifts For Her: negligee, half slip, camisole, costume jewelry, belt set, perfume, cosmetics, slippers, hostess robe, clothing storage bag, blow dryer, small clutch bag, travel-alarm clock.

- Personal Gifts For Him: monogrammed pajamas, robe, slippers, travel-alarm clock, shaving equipment, cuff links, traveling toilet case, tie rack, comb-and-brush set, clothing storage bags, blow dryer, wallet.

- Gift From The Group: toaster oven, blender, food processor, microwave, television set, wok set, toaster, portable vacuum cleaner, clock radio, lamp, card table and folding chairs, room divider, stack stools, stack tables, electric griddle, picnic basket with accessories, electric broom, shop vacuum, fireplace tools with canvas log-tote, one-time general housecleaning service, well-stocked tool box, drill, camping equipment, luggage, any substantial personal or personalized gift, barbecue set, dinner-for-two gift certificate, season tickets to opera, theater, symphony or sports event.

- Personalized gifts: engraved door knocker, paper weight, luggage tags, sterling bookmark, brass business card case or holder, silver bread and butter dishes, napkin rings, silverplated photo case, address labels, checkbook cover with stamped name, engraved key chain, personalized stationary, two inscribed champagne glasses, framed wedding invitation, initialed money clip, monogrammed sheets, pillow cases or towels.

- Miscellaneous: handmade articles (quilts, afghans, lingerie), brass or pewter items, health products (vitamins, herb teas, snacks), road atlas or travel books, auto-plate-holder.

GIFT WRAP GUIDE

IDEAS FROM SHOWER THEMES:

- Tie in shower gifts for business associates with a wrap that matches their profession or department . . . as in "Co-Worker" shower.
- When the wedding couple is apt to know what each gift package contains because of size or shape, turn-the-tables on them. Ask guests to use odd-sized boxes or to wrap in unusual ways. Then make a guessing game of it with everyone participating . . . as in "Wedding Registry" shower.

OTHER IDEAS:

- Buy personalized wrapping with the individual's name printed in stripes across the paper.
- Wrap large gifts in a paper tablecloth, either plain or with a wedding design.
- Use newspapers: Wall Street Journal for the executive; comics for a fun gift; grocery store ads for food gifts; hardware store ads for tools.
- Use wallpaper samples for a sturdy wrap, or shelf-lining for quick, last-minute wrapping.
- Purchase gift bags or make fabric drawstring sacks in the wedding party colors.
- Buy white boxes from a bakery and decorate with fancy ribbon or design them with colored marking pens.
- Make kitchen-towel cakes, kitchen-placemat cakes or bath cakes. Roll up cloths to resemble a layer cake. Or ask for The Cloth Bakery^{T.M.} cakes at your gift store. Much too pretty to wrap!
- Use large gifts as decorative wrapping for several smaller gifts: hamper with bathroom supplies; wicker basket with spices; laundry basket with grocery items.

PRIZES GUIDE

KITCHEN GADGET SUGGESTIONS

Pie server, oval roast-rack, double melon baller, plastic ladle, kitchen shears, pizza cutter, butter warmer, peg rack, measuring cup set, food server, hors d'oeuvres spreader, nylon scrubbers, vegetable peeler, cocktail forks, egg fry rings, two-way bottle caps, pastry blender, spaghetti tongs, napkin rings, magnetic hooks, apple divider, measuring spoon set, tomato slicer, acrylic honey twist, strawberry huller, whisk set, four-sided grater, garlic press, egg slicer, three-wheel pie crimper, scrapers, spatulas, funnel, plate hanger, Swedish meatballer, salad scissors, pastry brush, grapefruit spoons, ketchup saver, cookie spatula, set of scoops, can covers, cheese slicer, tea infuser, straw trivet, cake rack, soap octopus, hot pads.

PRIZE SUGGESTIONS FOR MEN-ONLY SHOWERS

Small tools, key chain, batteries, razor blades, flashlight, sweat bands, combs, playing cards, nail clipper, pens.

PRIZE SUGGESTIONS FOR WOMEN-ONLY SHOWERS

Scarf, perfume, combs, brush, teacup, head bands, purse organizer, herb teas, nail polish, sachet, box of all-occasion cards.

PRIZE SUGGESTIONS FOR A COUPLE'S SHOWER

Tennis or golf balls, small sports supplies (tees, sweat bands), mug, mirror, soap balls, change holder, book mark, sweat socks, shoe laces, tape measure, how-to books, carafe, coat hangers, jumbo clothes hook, feather duster, stationery supplies.

UNUSUAL LOCATIONS GUIDE

Most showers are held in the home or in VFW or similar club halls. Here are others for your consideration.

IDEAS FROM SHOWER THEMES:
- Country club or golf clubs . . . as in "The Elegant" shower.
- Supper club, patio restaurant or hotel/motel meeting rooms . . . as in "Second-Time-Around" shower.
- Office conference room, company lunch room or cafeteria . . . as in "Office Co-Worker" shower.
- Class room or locker room . . . as in "No-Sweat" and "Calorie-Counter" showers.

OTHER IDEAS:
- Enjoy the sunshine at a beach, lake or pool.
- Park yourself in a park or picnic area with clean-up facilities.
- Rent a yacht, paddle boat or houseboat.
- Rent a mansion, theater lobby or public cafeteria.
- "Borrow" a greenhouse or flower garden.

AFTER THE END . . .

We really can't say this book was exactly easy to write. After all, how would you feel about two active cupids flying yonder and fro . . . perching on desks and typewriters . . . hanging from umbrellas . . . shooting off arrows? And that was the good part.

No, it wasn't easy, but it WAS very enjoyable. We're sure cupids come in all shapes and sizes and ShowerWise were two of the best.

But, the book was finished and it was time to say good-bye. We knew we'd miss them. They'd become such a part of our lives. Besides, one thing bothered us. They didn't seem to mind leaving us behind at all.

"Come, come now." they grinned, "There will be no good-byes . . . not even fond farewells. These words aren't even in our vocabulary. There's just no need. For, if you listen closely," they whispered, "everytime a shower is held somewhere . . . anywhere . . . a tiny crystal bell will chime, 'Hello! Hello!.'"

We should have known.

SPECIAL NOTE FROM SHOWERWISE . .

"They" don't know it yet, but they'll be writing other books to help you. So, here's your chance to ask any baby shower, graduation party or children's party questions you may have. Just drop us a line and be sure to include a self-addressed, stamped envelope if you'd like an acknowledgement:

ShowerWise
c/o Brighton Publications, Inc.
P.O. Box 12706
New Brighton, MN 55112

And, how about sharing your good ideas on these subjects with other readers across the country?

Just think! YOUR name could be in our next book. You'll have fame, fortune . . . be on all the TV shows . . . welcomed everywhere!

They're right. We DO get carried away sometimes. Nevertheless . . . we'll be waiting to hear from YOU . . .

SHOWER THEME INDEX

APARTMENT/CONDO POOL   44
  SHOWER

BE-MY VALENTINE SHOWER   49
BIO-RHYTHM SHOWER   84

CALORIE-COUNTER SHOWER   65
CANDLELIGHT SHOWER   83
CHERISHED-GIFT SHOWER   79
CHRISTMAS-BAUBLE SHOWER   85
CO-HOSTESS SHOWER   69
COLLECTIBLE SHOWER   82
COLLEGE SOAP-OPERA SHOWER   37
COOKIE-SAMPLER SHOWER   41
CORNUCOPIA SHOWER   83

DOLLAR-DISCO-DANCE SHOWER   55

THE ELEGANT SHOWER   53
ENGLISH-TEA SHOWER   88
ERIN-GO-BRAGH SHOWER   88

FABULOUS-FORTIES SHOWER   84
FILE-AND-FIND-IT SHOWER   86
FORMAL POOL SHOWER   33

GERMAN SHOWER   87
GIFTS-AROUND-THE-CLOCK   80
  SHOWER
GIFT-THEME GALLERY   76
GREENHOUSE SHOWER   78

HANDY-ANDY/   42
  HARDWARE-HANNAH SHOWER
HAWAIIAN SHOWER   87
HEALTH-FOOD-HARVEST   85
  SHOWER
HERB-AND-SPICE SHOWER   83
HERITAGE THEME GALLERY   86
HOLLYWOOD STARS SHOWER   67
HOME-FROM-THE-   35
  HONEYMOON SHOWER

ITALIAN SHOWER   87

LAS VEGAS DICE-THROW   83
  SHOWER
LEND-A-HAND SHOWER   79
LET'S-GET-CANNED SHOWER   85

MEET-THE-RELATIVES   51
  SHOWER
MEXICAN SHOWER   86

NIFTY-FIFTIES SHOWER   84
NO-SWEAT SHOWER   71

OFFICE CO-WORKER SHOWER   60
OPEN-DOOR SHOWER   85
ORIENTAL SHOWER   87

POSTAL SHOWER   78
POUNDING-PARTY SHOWER   31

ROAST-THE-MANAGER SHOWER   47
ROMANTIC NOVEL SHOWER   73

SECOND-TIME-AROUND   39
  SHOWER
SCANDINAVIAN SHOWER   86
SHARE-A-MENU SHOWER   61
SHEET-MUSIC SHOWER   83
SHOW-ME SHOWER   24
SHOWER-ON-A-SHOESTRING   26
SONG-OF-INDIA SHOWER   88
SUNDAY-GO-TO-MEETING   29
  SHOWER
SURPRISE-FRIENDSHIP SHOWER   63

TAILGATE SHOWER   86
TIE-A-QUILT SHOWER   57

WEDDING REGISTRY SHOWER   77
WINE-AND-CHEESE-TASTING   27
  SHOWER
WOK-ON-THE-WILD-SIDE   74
  SHOWER

BOOKS AVAILABLE FROM:
BRIGHTON PUBLICATIONS, INC. . . .

"FOLDING TABLE NAPKINS: A New Look at a Traditional Craft" by Sharon Dlugosch.

"TABLE SETTING GUIDE" by Sharon Dlugosch

"FOOD PROCESSOR RECIPES FOR CONVENTIONAL AND MICROWAVE COOKING" by Sharon Dlugosch, Joyce Battcher.

"WEDDING SHOWER FUN" by Sharon E. Dlugosch, Florence E. Nelson

"GAMES FOR WEDDING SHOWER FUN" by Sharon E. Dlugosch, Florence E. Nelson

Write to Brighton Publications, Inc., P. O. Box 12706, New Brighton, Minnesota 55112, for ordering information.